Encore

WISCONSIN

chef's

recipes

designed

to

bring

you

ovations

by Grace Howaniec

Library of Congress Catalog Number: 92-74386

ISBN: 0-942495-18-7

For additional copies of this book, contact:

Amherst Press
A division of Palmer Publications, Inc.
P.O. Box 296
Amherst, Wisconsin 54406

Dedication

To BJ who has tasted it all—and cleaned up after me.
Your love and support have made this book possible.

Acknowledgments

Books are never just the product of one person's labor but a collective that begins with a good idea involving the inspiration and creative talents of many individuals. One way to thank them is to acknowledge them in a formal way, hopefully in print. Merci Beacoup!

My mother Inez Hinde who set me loose in her country kitchen at age seven and said, "Call me if you need me. I'll be at the clothes line." (I still call her when the jam doesn't jell or the rolls don't rise.)

My father, Glenn Hinde, who liked everything I ever cooked and fostered my love of words. Your confidence gave me courage and derring-do.

My test staff, Cheryl Slagter and Nancy Bong who approached testing these recipes with missionary fervor. It was a joy to work with you.

Mike Huibregtse and staff for their usual stellar photography. You make the food (and me) shine.

Mary Franz, a food stylist who brings dedication to detail and a wonderful sense of humor to every task.

Mike Falk and Mike Labinski, two young friends who unsnarled my computer and saved my sanity. I owe you many, many dinners.

My children, Jon and Anne—it has been my joy to feed you over the years. When can I come to dinner?

My family and friends who always felt I should do a cookbook. Here's the first one.

Roberta and Chuck Spanbauer—your love of food and appreciation of my efforts made this a joyful venture. Thank you for your confidence and patience.

Introduction

Encore—we say it each time we encounter something spectacular in the arts that demands a repeat performance. When food is the star, we salute the chefs. And in *Encore* WISCONSIN, our collection of chef's recipes designed to bring you ovations, we want to put the chef's hat on you, the home or hobbyist cook who would like to learn the secrets and techniques used in creating memorable meals and unforgettable dishes.

Inside this collection, you will find a wealth of culinary riches gathered from talented chefs around the state who willingly shared some of their most requested recipes with you, the readers. When chefs were asked to share signature dishes or recipes that are popular with their patrons, they did so, acknowledging that many are true "foods for feasting". These festive foods are richer in ingredients and flavor. They are the celebratory foods reserved for special occasions.

You will recognize many of the restaurants and be acquainted with the chefs and their reputations. Some are small family owned and operated businesses. Others are larger with multi-layered staffs. In each case, their food has brought them encores.

As we journeyed around the state and followed our culinary instincts, we undoubtedly missed some excellent places that should have been included in this volume. Our apologies if we missed your restaurant or inn, or if we were unable to include every tasty recipe that you sent us. Some recipes submitted were very similar and choosing between them was difficult.

Our mission, from the beginning, was to make you the star in your own kitchen. In order to place your chef's hat on comfortably and confidently, we tested each recipe to ensure the best possible results. Chef's recipes are frequently done in larger quantity than those done in home kitchens. Sizing down recipes for home use was one of the biggest challenges the test staff faced. In some instances, as in the case of the Toffee Crumbles, it was necessary to make a larger recipe than is required for the accompanying Heath Bar Pie. We have included tips for other uses for these and any other "leftovers".

You will find that some of the recipes are done quickly. Some have parts that may be done in advance. Others are labor-intensive but have explicit instructions to put you comfortably in the chef's hat. In using this cookbook, you will undoubtedly come to appreciate, as we did, the craft of the food professionals in Wisconsin who labor long hours in painstaking detail—because they love what they do.

We compiled this book because we have encountered some fabulous foods in Wisconsin restaurants and inns that we wanted to savor again—in our own kitchens. We wanted an encore performance. We suspect we are not alone. We put together what we hope is a collection of culinary treasures—recipes designed to win you ovations whenever and wherever you put on your chef's hat.

CONTENTS

Wandering Wisconsin—
One Cook's Tour

Explore and savor the edible treasures of Wisconsin's bountiful and beautiful tables! This is my travelogue, a very partial list of the places that brought me gastronomic pleasure. Use it as you travel the state and add to it as you seek out some of your own special places and food memories.

To begin (almost in my own backyard) there is *Benny's Kitchen* on Waukesha's Main Street. Housed in the ground floor of an old hotel, Chef Benny Smith turns out Cajun/Creole food that brings the authentic taste of New Orleans to Wisconsin's Dairyland. Small and unpretentious, this friendly eatery serves up classics like Red Beans and Rice, Jambalaya, Gumbo Muffaletta and some of the best catfish you'll find anywhere. It's an informal place where water is served in sturdy Mason jars and so are some of the foods (as in the tasty combination plate). Live music is featured nightly from 6:30 pm until closing. Music at Benny's is an eclectic mix—one night fiddle champions; another classical conservatory musicians. A total of 61 performers dish up happy music on various nights that includes folk, bluegrass and zydeco. Come for the food and stay for the music!

One of the best spots for lunch is just to the east of my home in a small mall bordering the edge of Brookfield. The *Continental Cafe* on Bluemound Road serves up some of the tastiest salads, in-house bakery and delightful dinners (menu changes daily) in the area. Owners Rob and Lisa Ferguson put the accent on fresh, wholesome ingredients—food you feel good about eating. Fresh muffins and scones are served daily and should not be missed. Desserts are rich and indulgent for those who crave something at meal's end. Casual and contemporary, the cafe is attractively decorated with original artwork which changes regularly. Exceptional house wines (all served by the glass) allow guests to sample from a wide variety of moderately-priced to upscale selections.

Milwaukee-bound? You'd better plan to stay for several meals. There is so much fine food in this lakeside jewel of a city that you can't just stay one day.

The most talked-about restaurant in Milwaukee may well be *Sanford Restaurant* in a pleasant residential neighborhood just on the edge of downtown. The owner/chef Sanford D'Amato continues to win honors in national culinary competitions and coverage in magazines from *Esquire*, *Bon Appetit* and *Food and Wine*. D'Amato was honored in 1991 as a James Beard Foundation nominee as Best Midwest Chef. Food and service in his intimate restaurant (50-person capacity) are as exquisite in flavor and presentation as his reviews and awards indicate. This is a special occasion restaurant where room must be saved for each peerlessly presented course from appetizer through dessert. Desserts are all individual servings and dazzle the eyes as well as the palate. D'Amato's menu changes several times a year and always reflects cuisine on the cutting edge. Don't miss it!

One of the newest stars on the Milwaukee dining scene is the popular, artistically decorated *Cafe Knickerbocker* close to Lake Michigan. Creativity and innovation mark the menu that features great pasta and main dish salads, wonderful fish entrees with herb-infused sauces and butters. A young culinary staff headed by Rob Wagner, a Johnson & Wales graduate, works as hard on standout flavors as they do on stellar presentation. A recently opened alfresco deck offers seating for 70 people during summer hours. This is East Side ambience at its best. Sunday brunch is also special.

Is it possible to move a long-standing popular family owned restaurant from a West Side location to the lakefront and keep your patrons happy? *The Boulevard Inn*, newly situated in the Cudahy Towers, would answer an emphatic, "yes". Consistently rated as one of Milwaukee's best restaurants, the Inn serves up time-treasured classics like Caesar Salad, Chicken Salad, and Schaum Tortes as well as delicate cold fruit soups and ethnic specialties like Pashka with Black Currants and Raspberry Sauce.

Classy surroundings featuring French windows, a dazzling chandelier, black and white floor tiles, cheery coral walls, potted palms and an abundance of gracious, round tables with comfortable upholstered chairs invite patrons to linger over leisurely, well-attended meals.

Traveling north out of Milwaukee on Highway 57, take the turn off on 23 and drive through picturesque Plymouth until you come to Stafford Street, right off of Main Street. An Irish Guest House, *52 Stafford*, listed on the National Register of Historic Places offers Irish warmth and hospitality in a beautifully refurbished 1892 inn. High ceilings, stained and leaded glass windows, and solid cherry mill work combine to create a congenial getaway guest house. The pub at the center of the inn is surely one of the most charming in America. Have a pint of Guinness, an exceptional Bloody Mary or hot Irish Coffee and for awhile you will feel yourself transported to the Emerald Island. Authentic Irish country fare like Colcannon and Guinness Brisket are mainstays on the menu that features fresh fish, seafood, poultry and meat entrees all prepared with great attention to detail.

If you are looking for the ultimate getaway—a place that soothes and satisfies in a hundred thoughtful ways—drive no farther than Kohler. Rich in history and European-style hospitality, *The American Club* resort in the village of Kohler transports you magically to a gentler, more gracious time. Exquisite attention to detail is a tradition in this beautifully restored hotel complex that is the Midwest's only resort to attain the American Automobile Association's coveted five diamond rating.

That standard of excellence carries into the American Club kitchens thanks to their creative staff of chefs. On New Year's Eve, several years ago, my husband and I enjoyed perhaps the best salmon entree of our lives in The Immigrant. Impeccably presented with two different colorful sauces, I have revisited the flavors of that entree many times in my mind. I have had similar, joyful culinary excursions in each of the resort dining areas. And always, save room for the exquisite dessert table offerings from the pastry chefs at The American Club. They are not to be missed.

Some places have personal romantic memories. Door County is one of those. Thirty-one years ago, a brash, young man from Chicago proposed to me in Peninsula State Park. Visiting the peninsula still makes me feel forever young—and just a little bit giddy.

Sturgeon Bay is the gateway to the peninsula and worth getting off the bypass to drive downtown to *The Inn At Cedar Crossing*. What began in 1985 as a bed-and-breakfast restoration in a century old brick building has blossomed into an architectural jewel listed on the National Register of Historic Places. The most recent expansion of the Inn includes a 95-seat full service restaurant that showcases elegant country cuisine in a beautifully restored dining room. The Inn also offers specialty bakery orders, picnic lunches and catering services.

Food is what keeps the trade so brisk and patrons so content at the Inn. From the beginning, Innkeeper Wulf, an avid promoter of Door County agriculture, has showcased locally grown produce and the freshest ingredients—all served on charming china with lovely linens. A fine place for breakfast, lunch or dinner and a great spot to rekindle romantic beginnings.

Back on Highway 42 heading north on the peninsula, the first village you visit is bustling Fish Creek. If you turn left, you will wander down treelined Main Street and may smell wood smoke, hear the crackle of open flames and watch an authentic peninsula Fish Boil. If you hear a few tunes being played on an accordion, you'll know that you are in the backyard of *The White Gull Inn* where Master Boiler Russ Ostrand not only cooks the fish but squeezes in a few tunes in the process.

The White Gull Inn has been a part of Fish Creek since 1896 and a historical treasure in the village. A favorite spot for visitors and locals alike, everything about the Inn charms visitors and guests. Sweeping flower-bedecked open porches, burnished wood floors and antiques, gracious hospitality and tasty peninsula food classics keep the Inn thriving. Owners Andy and Jan Coulson love to tell the tale that when they bought the Inn in 1972, there were only four recipes included in the sale. They were all Fish Boil recipes and the only culinary provisions they inherited. Happily for today's guests, that paucity of recipes has been replaced with a wealth of popular dishes that grow richer and more varied each year. Sample the Fish Boil or the Early American buffet. It is nearly unthinkable to visit Door County without enjoying the culinary wealth of The White Gull Inn.

On your way out of town, also on Main Street, you'll pass a charming restaurant called *The Cookery*. Try to plan your travels to include a meal here. Carol and Dick Skare have been operating their comfortable full service restaurant since July 4 of 1977 and their list of loyal patrons continues to grow. Carol's rural background sets the proper note for hearty breakfasts, substantial sandwiches, homemade soups and delicious in-house bakery. The dinner menu features daily specials and the adjoining Pantry gift shop offers The Cookery's own preserves and sauces as well as gift baskets and designer foods from all across Door County. If the Whitefish Chowder is on the menu, don't miss it!

Don't hurry through Sister Bay (although if the goats are grazing on the roof at Al Johnson's Restaurant the only speed is slow) but look for a side street called Maple Drive as you descend into the village. Tucked back around the corner, is *The White Apron*, a stovewood building listed in the National Register of Historic Places. This cozy inn with five guest rooms is open to the public for dinner and offers distinctive country dining with candlelight, fresh flowers and uncomplicated food. Barbara McCarrier, cook at The White Apron, features the best of locally produced fruits and vegetables, freshly caught and smoked fish from Lake Michigan and Wisconsin meats and cheeses.

Inn guests are invited to linger on the sun-dappled front porch or dining room over a leisurely breakfast of fresh fruits, pastries still warm from their own bakery and the inn's own blend of fresh ground coffee. You can walk from the inn to many of Sister Bay's shops and attractions—a plus for travelers who want to unwind.

Entering the Fox River Valley on Appleton's College Avenue, you have to find the Paper Valley Hotel in order to locate *Christie's* restaurant. It is tucked along the side of the huge hotel lobby and looks more like a proper gentleman's library than most private libraries do. Treat yourself to Shrimp Peking in Ginger Orange Sauce—transparent shrimp wrapped in fresh basil leaves and leek and wonton skins fried briefly to tempura-like lightness and served with a delicate sauce. Or order their Lamb Spring Green, a delicately seasoned boneless loin of lamb encased in a herb seasoned butterflied pork tenderloin. It's an ambrosial entree, served with a rosemary infused sauce. Their Spinach Salad is also memorable. Next time, I'll save room for dessert.

If you are searching for authentic tastes and culture of Mexico, you'll want to stop at *Lara's Tortilla Flats* in Oshkosh. Owner Ada Lara de Thimke proudly states that you will find no sleeping Mexican figures under sombreros decorating her tasteful interior and no cliches among her entrees. A gallery of family pictures featuring relatives involved in the Revolution, Mexican pottery and Diego Rivera posters mark her well-chosen art. And the influence of Great-Grandmother Theresa Moran who ran a boarding house in the mining town of Salinas can be found in some of the restaurant's popular entrees.

If you've never tasted cactus, try Lara's Nopalitos Con Queso. Also interesting is mole poblano (featuring more than twenty herbs and spices) or pipian. Desserts like Leche Bunuelos and Leche Quemada are designed for those who like authenticity in their food. And if Camarones Mazatlan, a Mexican version of shrimp cocktail, is on the menu, indulge yourself and try this pretty, tasty summertime treat.

Fisherman and boaters looking for a casual place to eat spurred the opening of *Norton's Marine Dining Room* on Green Lake in 1948. Food was simple at the beginning but did include Norton's well-known Shore Dinner served on Friday nights. Fish chowder cooked outdoors in blackened cast iron kettles, broiled or fried fish, bacon, cole slaw and pancakes made with real maple syrup made up the popular Shore dinner. Today, fish chowder and fish dinners on Friday night pay tribute to their Shore Dinner precursers

Much has changed at Norton's since the simple fare preferred by fishermen in early years. Large-scale remodeling of the dining room and kitchen, the addition of upscale menu entrees and a well-trained staff promised that lakeside dining at Norton's are a not to be missed treat when in the Green Lake area.

Just a short trip to the northwest brings us to *The Vintage* in Wisconsin Rapids. Owners Jim and Elly Jensen moved their restaurant operation into the brick and stone building that formerly housed Wilbern's Restaurant, a landmark for years in central Wisconsin. Their eclectic menu showcases the creative talents of Pastry Chef Amy Crowns and Chef Peter Jennings, who brainstorm daily for new menu ideas and the best use of seasonal foods. Regional foods like Blueberry Slumps and Creole Cheese Fritters share space with comfort foods like Braised Lamb Shanks with Balsamic Vinegar and Leek Mashed Potatoes. Owners Jim and Elly Jensen acknowledge that their menu tries to be as adventurous as their market will bear. Don't miss any of their stunning desserts. Their pies are winners and their Chocolate Turtle Cheesecake topped with Caramel and Walnuts should be sampled, too.

The center of the state has its edible treasures, too. For breakfast or lunch, you can stop at *The Kitchen Table* in Marshfield, a cozy 47-seat restaurant that exudes the warmth and friendliness of its owners Lloie and Stewart Schwartz. Opened in 1977, it was nicknamed "The Weird Food Place" by local experts who predicted it would last six months. Fifteen years later, the restaurant enjoys wide popularity among locals and visitors alike who love the omelets, soups, salads, sandwiches and desserts that are available Monday through Saturday. Food is mainly prepared on the premises from scratch with devotion to quality. (Even the bread is homemade, sans mixer.)

In tiny Hazelhurst, a young couple named Pam and Alan Jacobi took out a second mortgage on their home and took over the family business—in Alan's own words, a local tavern complete with pool table and juke box. Heavily armed with a shoe-string budget and an indomitable spirit, they set out to become a serious gourmet restaurant. Needless to say the local clientele didn't share their vision. They thought the Jacobi's had lost their senses. Seven years later, Jacobi's has put Hazelhurst on the culinary map. Their appetizers are extremely popular (and laboriously made by Pam and staff) and guests have come to prize their homemade soups and interesting entrees. Stop in at *Jacobi's of Hazelhurst* to taste and see what can happen if you dare to follow your (culinary) dreams.

While you are overlooking the Apostle Islands in Bayfield, it would be a shame not to hop a ferry to Madeline Island and follow the rumors of exceptional cuisine offered by Chef James Webster at *The Clubhouse*. This seasonally open island restaurant with a maximum seating of 80 people offers the best views of the island from its dining room. The uniquely designed 12-sided building features panoramic water views from its expansive windows. Chef Webster, who learned his trade in St. Paul restaurants, changes the menu once a month and prides himself in using as much locally grown organic produce as the nearby cornucopia can provide. His wine list is discriminating and exceptionally well-chosen. Because the season is short, special events fill the summer calendar with Vineyard Wine dinners, Music Camp Concerns and annual spring and harvest dinners.

I had read about *The Old Rittenhouse Inn* in lovely Bayfield in all the travel and lifestyle magazines and couldn't wait to see it for myself. Friends had invited us to be a part of a Murder Mystery Weekend at the Inn and we were delighted to find that our group had taken over all the guest suites in the magnificent LeChateau Boutin. As the evening drama unfolded around the antique dining table, six stunning courses were served in delightfully timed interludes. The star of the dinner may well have been the fresh ginger-laced Cranberry Sorbet but I do not recall leaving any morsel of food on my various plates.

Breakfast the next morning in The Old Rittenhouse proper offered a variety of tempting breakfast options always accompanied by some perfect sauce or preserves, handmade in the Inn kitchens. Chef Mary Phillips and her inspired staff keep their offerings fresh and on the cutting edge. Local fruits and produce, an abundance of fresh herbs and fish from the ice cold waters of Lake Superior inspire their cuisine. Include The Old Rittenhouse Inn in your culinary travels.

If you drive south from Bayfield to Mikana, Wisconsin, you'll have to take the boat to get to *Stout's Lodge on the Island of Happy Days* but I recommend the trip. Years ago, my brothers and sisters sent my parents there to celebrate a late-in-life wedding anniversary and my mother still recalls the romantic picnic lunch that the staff packed for them while they were guests.

Chef Scott Maanum offers exquisite cuisine in the Island Dining Room featuring island-grown fresh herbs, vegetables and locally grown produce and game. His full-service menu for guests changes daily. Their friendly brochure offers explicit directions for driving to the boat launch but then adds comfortingly, "Call us if you get lost."

With breathtaking views of the Chippewa River Valley below, *Fanny Hill* restaurant and bed-and-breakfast in Eau Claire may well have one of the prettiest spots for a country inn in the state of Wisconsin. Its Victorian architecture holds seven delightfully refurbished rooms and an in-house dinner theatre.

Food is the star here with Executive Chef, John Mazzei, a graduate of the Baltimore Culinary Institute specializing in innovative dishes that utilize native Wisconsin products like cranberries and walleye in upscale desserts and entrees. Fanny Hill has a prized Four Diamond rating by AAA for its accommodations and service. If Chef Mazzei offers his Cranberry and Granny Smith Apple Bread Pudding Cake with Grand Marnier Cream during one of your visits, save room for it.

I have biked along the Red Cedar River to reach *The Creamery* in the small town of Downsville and driven there with a car filled with hungry relatives. However you get there, the trip is worthwhile. Nestled in the rolling hills of Western Wisconsin farmland, The Creamery is an unexpected find. Originally a cooperative creamery that produced butter, the Thomas family acquired the building and opened the restaurant in 1985.

Imaginative American cuisine featuring seasonal, fresh ingredients has become the trademark of The Creamery. Wonderful salads and interesting entrees mark their menu. Their wine cellar features a large selection of vintage California wines, and champagnes are available for special occasions. Live music is featured in the lounge. A garden terrace and surrounding flower gardens provide a relaxing counterpoint to life's cares.

My first visit to the *Harbor View Cafe* in the tiny river town of Pepin was memorable. My sister had heard of their incredible food and without a map and with nearby roads under construction, we set out to celebrate my birthday dinner. Hours later, a bit dustier from the trip (and definitely hungrier) we settled ourselves in the comfortable booths of this bustling riverfront cafe. One of my sisters ordered a Pork Chop with Rhubarb Sauce; one ordered fresh salmon; one had Morels on Toast Points. We all had dessert, and it was all delicious. It was fun and festive, and I remember it as one of the happiest birthdays of my life.

Go there to celebrate any of life's special occasions. Be prepared to wait for a table in their busy season. You can tour this picturesque town on foot or browse in their adjacent bookstore while waiting.

I think I'd like to go to *Susie's Restaurant* in Baraboo and stay for about a week and just systematically eat my way through her famous "celebration of fresh foods" menu and then nap contentedly for a few days after. How many times do you find a small-town restaurant that features Croissant French Toast with Zest of Orange and Triple Sec, Smoked Salmon and Cream Cheese Omelets, Vegetarian Stir-Frys, Sautéed Marlin with Honey Dill Sauce, Brittany Cod Bake or Black Bean Burritos? And we haven't even touched on baker Will Clark's scrumptious breads or to-die-for-desserts like Heath Bar Pie and honest-to-goodness homemade Apple Pie served with Cinnamon Sauce.

Susie's offers road-weary interstate travelers a reason to pull off the highway and refresh themselves in tastefully decorated surroundings complete with soothing semi-classical music, fresh flowers, crisp linens and no smoking anywhere. In the process you will sample fare that is affordable, fresh and filled with pleasant surprises. Susie, the ebullient blonde owner will greet you warmly and hum in tune as she seats you. This is a restaurant of many pleasures, worth a detour to savor.

One of my favorite Wisconsin cities for dining is Madison. With two children at various times at the University, there have been ample opportunities to savor all manner of fare in this charming capital city.

One of the loveliest and most unforgettable meals of my life was at *L'Etoile*, the intimate, second-story restaurant on Madison's Capitol Square. My daughter, Anne, and I shared her first pâté at a window table overlooking the Capitol, brillantly bathed in night light. Every detail of the meal was perfect. When we left several hours later, feeling nourished by our experience, I remember telling my wide-eyed daughter that she had probably just eaten one of the most memorable meals of her lifetime.

That experience is one that Chef/Owner Odessa Piper strives for in her exquisite, critically acclaimed restaurant on the east side of Capitol Square. Since she opened her restaurant in 1976, Piper has concentrated on locally produced foods handled with creativity and respect. She and Co-Chef Eric Rupert draw up their weekly menus as a team, each contributing ideas and inspirations from free associations of foods that they encounter in their daily lives. A must for anyone who appreciates fine food.

Just several blocks to the south of the square is another delightful find. We discovered *Wilson Street Grill* on a snowy December night after a harrowing drive from Milwaukee through a winter storm. My husband's eyes were as glazed as the roads we had just traveled, and we desperately needed rest and some nourishing sustenance. Friends had recommended the Grill to us and it sounded perfect for our casual, winter-wise attire.

We stumbled into the warmth of this contemporary eatery and dissolved into the comfort of its attractive surroundings. Appealing artwork, excellent service and stunning flavors calmed our road weary bodies and rested frayed nerves. We sampled Goat Cheese Focaccia, Italian Clam Chowder and several different grilled entrees and purred over every satisfying mouthful created by the talented chef's team of Christy and Craig. Grilled foods are the restaurant's specialty that showcases a wide variety of vegetables, meats, fish and poultry that benefit from tasty marinades and perfect grilling techniques. Check it out—and don't wait for a snowstorm.

On the outskirts of Madison you will find *Quivey's Grove*, a lovely four acre country estate that you may have read about in lifestyle publications including *Midwest Living* magazine. Beautifully restored by owner Joseph Garton, the 135 year old Stone House is the star of the estate that includes a Stable Tap & Grill, a paddock and charming tree lined grounds. Five dining rooms in the mansion are decorated nostalgically featuring antique quilts, hand stenciling, vintage lighting fixtures and authentic pine and walnut furnishings.

Start your outing in the Stable Tap & Grill with beverage or appetizer and then walk through the 60-foot long tunnel that leads from the Grill to the Stone House for dinner. History finds its way into the menu with entrees honoring Wisconsin notables from composer Carrie Bond to the father of urban planning, John Nolan. Master Chef Craig Kuenning spotlights the area's legacy of Scandinavian and German dishes and uses the best of Wisconsin's ingredients like sweet butter, fresh fish and seasonal berries in his offerings. This is the place to celebrate a special occasion and is beautiful no matter what season.

My "foodie" friends have recommended *The Red Geranium* in Lake Geneva for its charming country inn atmosphere, excellent service and outstanding food. My only regret about this lovely restaurant is that it took me so long to discover its multiple pleasures. The exterior of the restaurant is inviting, surrounded with its white picket fence, perfectly groomed masses of bright red geraniums and gracious sprawling like-home design. Inside everything is light (from masses of nicely spaced bay windows), bright (from white walls stenciled with clusters of red geraniums) and spacious with high ceilings and well-placed ficus trees.

Happily, the food is just as appealing and delicious. Daily specials, including grilled fish or seafood—a specialty of the restaurant—with innovative accompaniments and sauces are printed along with helpful wine suggestions for each entree. The regular menu is not overly large but is consistently excellent whether you order the Grilled Lamb Chops Provencal or the Salmon Fillet with Raspberry Beurre Blanc Sauce. Salad dressings are all homemade and delicious. Raspberry Yogurt with a dash of mustard is a delightful taste sensation. A friend and I split an appetizer order of Escargots (some of the best I have ever tasted) and also divided their warm Flourless Chocolate Cake served on a pool of Raspberry Melba with a dollop of whipped cream. Serving this dessert warm was inspired as the texture was soft and tender—unlike many flourless chocolate cakes I have sampled. When you are in the Lake Geneva area, do remember to sample the multiple charms of The Red Geranium restaurant.

Leaving the Lake Geneva area, I can easily stop for lunch or dinner at *Heaven City Restaurant* in Mukwonago. Originally built as a Spanish-style home for a wealthy tobacco dealer, Heaven City consists of a variety of dining rooms surrounding an atrium-like center, replete with interesting structural details. There is a separate room provided for pipe and cigar smokers who enjoy either after a meal. But it is the glorious food of Chef Scott McGlinchey that keeps patrons content—and coming back. Appetizers are innovative and shouldn't be missed. This is a restaurant where I save room for courses knowing that I will want to sample flavors from starters through dessert. One of my personal favorites among luncheon choices is the Grilled Lamb Salad with Rosemary Dressing. For dessert, Warm Apple Tart with Caramel Sauce is absolutely flawless.

Waukesha County's Lake Country abounds with pretty restaurants that serve fine food. Among my favorites is the ***Red Circle Inn*** in tiny Nashotah. History buffs may know that this is Wisconsin's oldest restaurant which had its beginning in 1848 as a stagecoach stop and hotel for weary travelers along Watertown Plank Road. Over its 140 year old history, the Inn has hosted fur traders, farmers, wealthy midwestern families, Badger football fans and Lake Country residents with discriminating palates.

Newly remodeled in 1989 and under the management of Renee and Mark Manion, the Red Circle Inn continues its long-standing tradition of gracious hospitality and elegant dining in a nostalgic country setting. Provimi veal and lamb, as well as top quality seafood and steaks are found on their menu that showcases American cuisine. The accent is on the freshest of ingredients from appetizers through desserts. All breads and desserts are baked by their pastry chef on the premises. Beautiful garden and patio reception facilities are available for groups of 20 to 300. Don't forget the Red Circle Inn when planning a special occasion.

Tours must end. The body decrees it and time and the pocketbook concur. But the traveler returns home enriched and nourished by the honest, yet exquisite food that is characteristic of Wisconsin's culinary diversity.

APPETIZERS

Fresh Snow Pea Pods	12
with Garlic Cream Cheese and Horseradish Sauce	
Pico de Gallo	13
(Fresh Salsa)	
Grilled Asparagus	14
with Toasted Sesame Seeds, Garlic and Sherry Vinegar	
Baked Camembert Cheese	16
with Cranberry Chutney	
Baked Brie Appetizer	17
with Apples and Walnuts	
Shrimp Peking	18
with Ginger Orange Sauce	
Camarones Mazatlan	19
Grilled Pear and Roquefort Tart	20
with Caramelized Onions and Walnuts	
Asiago Cheese, Walnut and Caramelized Onion Ravioli	22
Anticuchos	24
with Guacamole	
Smoked Trout Turnovers	25
Norwegian Salmon Appetizer	26
with Watercress & Chive Vinaigrette	

Fresh Snow Pea Pods
with Garlic Cream Cheese
and Horseradish Sauce

makes 4 servings

Pea Pods:

4 cups fresh pea pods, washed,
  and drained

Sauce:

2 tablespoons plus 2 teaspoons
  horseradish
1 package cream cheese
  (8 ounces), softened
2 tablespoons plus 2 teaspoons
  dairy sour cream
1 teaspoon minced garlic
2 teaspoons ketchup
⅛ teaspoon (generous)
  Cayenne pepper
⅛ teaspoon (generous) salt

Chef Steven Smith's quick, vegetarian appetizer is colorful, crunchy and loaded with flavor. Keep this recipe in mind during holiday entertaining when guests look for something on the lighter side. The zesty sauce may be used with a variety of other crudités including julienne jicama, celery or bell peppers.

Snap off stem ends and pull string down to tip; discard ends and string. Place cleaned pea pods in ice water in large bowl and refrigerate for at least 2 hours or overnight.

Squeeze out any excess water from horseradish. Add horseradish to a small mixing bowl or bowl of food processor and add cream cheese, sour cream, garlic, ketchup, Cayenne pepper and salt. Process or mix for 1 minute, only occasionally scraping down sides of bowl. Chill, covered, for 2 hours in refrigerator.

Drain ice water from pea pods; place pea pods on several layers of paper toweling. Pat dry. Arrange around outside edge of glass serving platter. Place sauce in small bowl in center of platter.

CRANDALL'S RESTAURANT
640 West Washington Avenue
Madison, Wisconsin

Pico de Gallo

(Fresh Salsa)

makes 4 servings

2 large tomatoes, diced
2 small yellow onions, diced
16 sprigs fresh cilantro, chopped
6 fresh jalapeno peppers,
  seeded, membranes removed,
  diced*
1 tablespoon fresh lemon juice
Salt to taste

This is a delightfully simple salsa to make and a Lara's restaurant favorite. It is zesty, hot, crunchy and very fresh tasting. It is best to not let it sit for too long as the ingredients tend to lose their crunch. This is a relish and should not be soupy.

Combine all ingredients in a medium glass bowl; mix well. Serve with fresh tortilla chips, fresh hot tortillas and grilled cheese (queso fundido) or grilled meats.

* *When working with hot peppers, wear kitchen gloves. Wash hands thoroughly with soap and cool water when done.*

LARA'S TORTILLA FLATS
715 North Main Street
Oshkosh, Wisconsin

Grilled Asparagus
with Toasted Sesame Seeds, Garlic, and Sherry Vinegar

makes 4 servings

½ cup white sesame seeds (divided)

1 pound fresh asparagus, medium thickness, cut to 6-inch lengths

1 tablespoon plus 1½ teaspoons olive oil, extra-virgin is best (divided)

2 large cloves garlic, finely minced

1½ teaspoons light soy sauce

1½ tablespoons sherry vinegar

½ teaspoon white pepper

1 teaspoon dark roasted sesame oil, oriental style

4 thinly sliced lemon wedges—garnish

Asparagus is a springtime favorite at the Clubhouse. This light, savory appetizer takes advantage of the fresh, succulent taste of early season asparagus without overpowering its delicate nature. Also, crisply sautéed, fresh shiitake mushrooms make an excellent garnish. Grilling the asparagus imparts a pleasant smokiness, but this step may be eliminated if impractical says Chef Webster.

In a medium-sized non-stick sauté pan, toss ½ cup sesame seeds over medium heat until lightly browned, about 4 minutes. Immediately remove from heat and pour onto cold, dry plate. Set aside to cool.

Bring 4 quarts of lightly salted water to boil in large kettle. Blanch asparagus in boiling water for 3-4 minutes and quickly plunge into ice cold water to prevent further cooking. Drain when cool; pat dry. (Asparagus should be tender, but very crisp.) Coat spears evenly with 1 tablespoon olive oil; grill for 2-3 minutes over high charcoal heat. Keep warm.

THE CLUBHOUSE
ON MADELINE ISLAND
Bayfield, Wisconsin

In a wok or large non-stick sauté pan, heat remaining 1½ teaspoons olive oil over high heat. When hot, add garlic; reduce heat to moderate. Sauté garlic for 2 minutes, being careful not to burn it. Add soy sauce, vinegar, and white pepper. Increase heat to high and reduce liquid by half, about 1-2 minutes.

Add asparagus and sesame oil and toss continually until heated through (pan should be nearly dry at this point). Over high heat, add ¼ cup sesame seeds to pan and toss until asparagus is evenly coated. (Having a nearly dry pan ensures crunchiness of sesame seeds.)

Arrange sesame coated asparagus spears on 4 heated plates. Garnish with ¼ cup remaining toasted sesame seeds and thinly sliced lemon wedges.

Baked Camembert Cheese
with Cranberry Chutney
makes 6 servings

Baked Camembert:
½ cup dried, finely ground
  bread crumbs
1½ teaspoons minced fresh
  parsley
1½ teaspoons sesame seeds
½ teaspoon ground basil
¼ teaspoon ground oregano
1 egg
¼ cup milk
1 wheel Camembert cheese
  (4 ounces)
2 tablespoons flour
Thin, toasted slices of French
  bread

Cranberry Chutney:
2 cups frozen cranberries
¾ cup cranberry juice
2 cups chopped pecans
1 cup sugar
1 tablespoon ground cinnamon
1 tablespoon nutmeg
1 cup water

An outstanding, quick appetizer from the repertoire of Chef William Gottsacker, owner/chef of City Streets Riverside Restaurant in Sheboygan. Creamy baked cheese inside a herb-crumb topping is perfectly accentuated by a homemade Cranberry Chutney. Pretty and delicious!

Prepare cheese by combining bread crumbs, parsley, sesame seeds, basil, oregano on a paper plate; mix well. Set aside. In a small mixing bowl, beat egg until blended; add milk. Dredge camembert in flour; then dip in egg mixture to coat cheese. Cover with bread crumb mixture.

Place crumb-topped cheese in small, shallow casserole dish. Bake in preheated oven at 350° until creamy or until cheese begins to melt, about 15 minutes. Serve with thin slices of toasted French bread and cranberry chutney.

Make chutney by combining all ingredients in heavy-bottomed medium saucepan. Bring to a boil over medium/high heat; reduce heat and simmer for 20 minutes, stirring occasionally. Chill thoroughly. Makes 4 cups.

**CITY STREETS
RIVERSIDE RESTAURANT**
*712 Riverfront Drive
Sheboygan, Wisconsin*

Baked Brie Appetizer
with Apples and Walnuts

makes 4 servings

1 cup unsalted butter (divided)
2 Granny Smith apples, peeled,
    cored and cut into ¼-inch bite-
    size pieces
1 cup chopped walnuts
4 sheets phyllo dough, about 14
    x 18 inches
8 ounces Brie cheese
Fresh parsley or
    chives—garnish

MAIN STREET BISTRO
340 Main Street
Racine, Wisconsin

If you look for appetizers that can be made in advance (and who doesn't?), keep these tasty morsels from Chef Tom Kenny in mind. They can be made up to two days in advance and stored, following his directions, in the refrigerator. The trio of apple, walnut, and cheese flavors is delightful.

In a 9-inch diameter skillet or sauté pan, melt 6 tablespoons of butter, add apples and walnuts and sauté over medium heat until apples begin to soften, about 5 minutes. Remove from heat; cool.

Peel off 4 sheets of phyllo dough (do not separate). Divide the dough into four quarters, each measuring about 7 x 8½ inches. Melt the remaining butter. With a pastry brush, coat the edges of phyllo dough rectangles with butter. Place ¼ cup apple walnut mixture in center of each phyllo rectangle. Then add 2 ounces of cheese and 2 more tablespoons apple walnut mixture.

Fold dough over once lengthwise carefully enclosing filling. Fold in both sides and fold lengthwise edges over side folds to seal. Brush melted butter under edges of folds and over top of entire pastry. Brush a little melted butter on a small baking sheet. Place all four portions on pan and bake in a preheated 350° oven for 10 minutes or until golden brown. Garnish with parsley or chives.

(These can be made up to two days ahead and stored in the refrigerator. They must be stored on a floured pan to avoid sticking. Do not cover directly with plastic wrap as it will stick to the dough. Tent the covering to avoid clinging to dough.)

Shrimp Peking
with Ginger Orange Sauce

makes 2 servings

Sauce:

1 teaspoon chopped fresh ginger
¼ cup brandy
½ cup freshly squeezed orange
    juice, strained
1 cup mayonnaise

Shrimp:

8 large raw shrimp (21-25 count
    size), peeled and deveined
8 wonton wrappers
8 fresh basil leaves
2 medium leeks (white bulb only)
    cut in julienne (about 2
    teaspoons)
2 eggs, beaten
Vegetable oil for deep-fat frying

Almost transparent with its delicate wonton skin wrapper, this basil and leek wrapped shrimp adds new meaning to the perfect appetizer. This offering is from Executive Chef Chuck Schuster and Sous Chef Terry Rathsack.

Make sauce by mixing together ginger, brandy, orange juice and mayonnaise in small bowl with electric mixer on low speed. Whip for 2 minutes. Put in refrigerator for at least 2 hours to blend flavors.

Butterfly shrimp by making an ⅛-inch deep cut with sharp paring knife along center back of shrimp; spread two halves open. Stuff each shrimp with 1 basil leaf and ½ teaspoon leek.

Wrap shrimp in wonton wrapper, leaving tail exposed. Brush all edges of wonton with beaten egg; press firmly to seal. Set aside.

Heat oil for deep-fat frying in suitable container to 350°. Carefully slip wontons into hot fat and fry for 1½ minutes. Remove to drain thoroughly on paper towels.

Place a small pool of ginger sauce on each serving plate. Place shrimp on top of pooled sauce. This may be served as an appetizer or lunch entree. Garnish, if desired, with a fresh sprig of basil or strips of orange zest.

CHRISTIE'S
333 West College Avenue
Appleton, Wisconsin

Camarones Mazatlan

makes 4 servings

1¼ cups diced tomato
½ cup diced onion
4 tablespoons diced green olives
4 tablespoons chopped fresh
   cilantro
½ teaspoon dried leaf oregano,
   crumbled
2 teaspoons fresh lemon juice
¼ cup ketchup
2 cups prepared seafood cocktail
   sauce
1¼ pounds medium shrimp,
   cooked, shelled, deveined and
   chopped
12 large shrimp, cooked, shelled,
   deveined, leave whole
8 leaves romaine lettuce,
   washed and chilled
4 lengthwise slices
   avocado—garnish
4 slices of escabeche (hot and
   spicy marinated
   carrot)—garnish
4 sprigs of fresh
   cilantro—garnish

Lara's Tortilla Flats offers its own version of shrimp cocktail on special occasions. This works great as a salsa with corn chips, as well.

Combine tomato, onion, olives, chopped cilantro, oregano, lemon juice, ketchup, cocktail sauce and chopped medium shrimp; mix well in medium bowl.

Garnish the bottom and one side of four 10-ounce Catalina glasses with lettuce. Divide shrimp mixture and place ¼ in each glass and top with garnishes of avocado, carrot and cilantro sprig. Top each with 3 large shrimp.

Serve chilled with bilillos (small loaves of crusty French-style bread found in Mexican markets) or crackers of your choice.

LARA'S TORTILLA FLATS
715 North Main Street
Oshkosh, Wisconsin

Grilled Pear and Roquefort Tart
with Caramelized Onions and Walnuts

makes 4 servings

Tarts:

4 puff pastry shells (4-inch
   diameter, ½ inch high)

Filling:

1 cup onions, peeled, cored,
   halved and sliced with grain
   as thin as possible
4 tablespoons butter, clarified*
   (divided)
1 tablespoon olive oil
2 tablespoons red wine vinegar
Pinch of freshly ground black
   pepper
⅛ teaspoon salt
1 Bartlett or D'anjou pear
   (8 ounces) semi-firm, peeled,
   halved and cored
Lemon juice
4 ounces cold Roquefort cheese,
   crumbled
4 tablespoons toasted and
   coarsely chopped walnuts
2 tablespoons walnut oil
4 pinches freshly ground black
   pepper

SANFORD RESTAURANT
1547 North Jackson
Milwaukee, Wisconsin

This stunning appetizer (much of which can be made ahead) is a wonderful example of flavor combinations that work well together as perfected by Chef Sanford D'Amato.

Bake pastry shells, covered with foil and filled with pie weights (or dry beans) in removable bottom tart pan in a preheated 350° oven for 8-10 minutes until light brown. Set aside to cool.

*To clarify butter melt 4 tablespoons butter in small saucepan over low heat. When completely melted, remove from heat, let stand for about 5 minutes allowing the milk solids to settle to the bottom. Skim the foamy white butterfat from the top; discard. Spoon off the clear yellow liquid— this is the clarified butter. Discard milk solids on bottom of pan. You should have about 3 tablespoons clarified butter for your use in this recipe.

Heat 8-inch diameter sauté pan until pan is very hot, about 3 minutes. Add 1 tablespoon clarified butter and oil; wait until oil starts to smoke. Carefully add onion, stirring immediately with a wooden spoon. Continue stirring as needed for about 20 minutes (onions should be golden without having burned specks on them). Add vinegar, salt and pepper and reduce until mixture is dry. Set aside. This mixture can be made ahead.

Cut each pear half in 6 fans (12 pieces total). Squeeze a little lemon juice over fans to hold color. Toss pear fans in 2 tablespoons clarified butter.

Place pear fans on hot grill or in non-stick pan and quickly brown over medium/high heat on each side. Set aside. This can be made ahead.

To assemble tart, place a thin layer of onions on bottom of each shell. Place ¼ of cheese on top of onions. Place 3 pear fans on top. Sprinkle ¼ of walnuts and walnut oil over pear and add one pinch of black pepper to each tart.

Bake in preheated 375° oven for 6-8 minutes until heated through. Serve with a small salad of arugula and fresh sorrel leaves with lemon and oil dressing.

Asiago Cheese, Walnut and Caramelized Onion Ravioli

makes 5-7 servings

Filling:

8 tablespoons unsalted butter (divided)
1 small onion, thinly sliced
2 tablespoons sugar
8 ounces Asiago cheese
¼ cup toasted chopped walnuts (roast 5-10 minutes in 400° oven)

Ravioli:

15-20 fresh pasta sheets or wonton wrappers, 4-inch square
1 large egg beaten with 2 teaspoons water

Accompaniments:

2 large Idaho russet potatoes, cut fine julienne (shoestring thickness)
Canola or corn oil for deep frying
1-2 teaspoons coarsely chopped fresh herbs (any combination of sage, parsley, basil, thyme)
3-4 quarts boiling water
Salt to taste
Freshly ground pepper to taste
Fresh herb sprigs—garnish

According to Chef James L. Webster, appetizers always seem to be among the most popular items on the Clubhouse menu and this recipe for ravioli is no exception. Over the seasons, the Clubhouse has offered many different pasta dishes, but this one receives, by far, the greatest number of requests.

Chef Webster acknowledges that while the procedure for this recipe is somewhat time consuming, the ravioli can be made in advance, frozen and kept in the freezer for up to one week until needed. If desired, the browned herb butter may be omitted. If Asiago (an aged cheddarlike Italian cheese) is unavailable, a good blue cheese, although dissimilar in taste and texture, makes a good substitution. Also, pecans work well in place of the walnuts.

THE CLUBHOUSE ON MADELINE ISLAND
Bayfield, Wisconsin

In a small non-stick saucepan, melt 2 tablespoons butter over medium heat. Add onions and sugar; cook, stirring frequently, until onions are soft and caramelized, about 15 minutes. Set aside. While onions are cooling, grate cheese coarsely and mix with toasted walnuts. Blend in cooled onions. Set aside.

Brush one diagonal half of pasta square with egg wash. Place about ½ ounce (1 tablespoon) of cheese mixture in center of square. Fold pasta over diagonally and press edges firmly. Crimp edges with pastry cutter wheel. Continue to fill remaining squares accordingly. Cover ravioli and refrigerate until needed.

Rinse sliced potatoes in three changes of cold water. Drain well; pat dry with clean towel. Deep fry in oil that has been heated to 375° and fry until crisp and golden. (Fried potatoes may be kept up to one day in covered, airtight container at room temperature.)

Cook ravioli in rapidly boiling water for about 3-5 minutes (in at least three batches to prevent sticking). Drain well; place on heated plates.

This browned herb butter is optional. Heat remaining 6 tablespoons butter in sauté pan until just golden brown and nutty tasting. Add herbs and a pinch of salt and pepper. (Herbs will fry and become crisp.) Remove from heat immediately and pour evenly over ravioli.

Top ravioli with a generous sprinkling of fried potatoes and garnish with sprigs of fresh herbs.

Anticuchos
with Guacamole
makes 4 servings

Marinade:

1 bunch of cilantro leaves,
   about ½ cup loosely packed
2 cups olive oil
1½ tablespoons chopped fresh
   garlic
½ teaspoon white pepper

Tuna/Chicken:

1 whole chicken breast (8
   ounces), skinned, boned
1 tuna steak (8 ounces), cut ½-
   inch thick

Guacamole:

6 ripe avocados, peeled, pit
   removed
½ cup finely diced onion
2 teaspoons chopped fresh
   garlic
1 tomato, seeded and diced
   fine
¼ cup fresh lime juice, about ½
   lime
1 teaspoon salt
4 Serrano peppers*, diced very
   fine
¼ cup loosely packed cilantro
   leaves, chopped fine

CLUB CHA CHA
1332 West Lincoln Avenue
Milwaukee, Wisconsin

My husband and I enjoyed this simple-to-make but tasty appetizer during our first visit to Club Cha Cha. Chef Scott McGlinchey likes the simple marinade that flavors the fresh tuna and/or chicken. This is a tasty way to introduce fresh tuna to family or friends.

Combine marinade ingredients in bowl of food processor. Process until well-blended. Set aside. Cut chicken breast in 4 equal pieces and tuna in 2 ounce cuts. Place chicken pieces and tuna pieces on individual skewers in flat dish and pour marinade over all. Marinate for at least 1 hour.

Mash avocados with fork on large flat plate. (Mixture will still have some lumps—this is the proper texture.) Add onion, garlic, tomato, lime juice, salt, peppers and cilantro. Mix together to blend. Place in serving bowl, cover tightly with plastic wrap until time to serve.

Grill drained skewers of chicken and tuna over hot coals or high on gas grill about 5 minutes per side. Remove to heated serving plate. Serve with Guacamole. Any leftover Guacamole can be used with crisp corn chips.

* Handle Serrano peppers carefully, using rubber gloves during chopping. Avoid touching face or eyes. Wash hands thoroughly with soap and water when finished.

Smoked Trout Turnovers

makes 6 servings

1 tablespoon diced shallots
1 tablespoon unsalted butter
3 ounces dry white wine
¼ cup coarse ground mustard
¾ cup heavy whipping cream
1 pound smoked trout
1 sheet of puff pastry, 10x10
   inches
1 egg, beaten
6 slices whole milk mozzarella
   cheese

Rushing Waters Trout Farm in Palmyra headed by Bill Johnson is, according to Chef Scott McGlinchey, the finest in the country, if not the world. A combination of specialized breeding, crystal spring waters and special organic diet produces the best Rainbow hybrid that McGlinchey has ever tasted. Bill smokes some of this fine fish and comes up with great, taste-tempting flavors. At Heaven City, this premier product is used to create an appetizer that is enormously popular with their patrons.

Make Shallot Sauce by sautéing shallots in butter over medium heat until translucent, about 2 minutes. Add wine; reduce volume by one-half, about 10 minutes. Stir in mustard and cream and heat thoroughly. Set aside.

Completely bone and flake trout fillets; set aside. Roll out puff pastry to 12-inch x 18-inch rectangle and cut into six, 6-inch squares. Brush pastry squares with beaten egg. Cut mozzarella slices on the diagonal and place in one corner of pastry.

Divide trout equally into 6 portions and place on top of cheese. Place other half of cheese slice on top of trout. Fold dough over filling and seal edges by pressing pastry edges tightly with a fork. Brush top of turnover with remaining egg wash. Bake in preheated 425° oven until golden brown, about 10-12 minutes.

Place a small pool of mustard sauce on each plate. Arrange turnover in center of pool. Serve immediately.

HEAVEN CITY RESTAURANT
S91 W27850 National Avenue
Mukwonago, Wisconsin

Norwegian Salmon Appetizer
with Watercress & Chive Vinaigrette
makes 8-12 servings

Court Bouillon:
1 quart water
3¾ cups white wine
½ cup fresh lemon juice
10 parsley stems (leaves stripped
   and reserved for vinaigrette)
1 tablespoon black peppercorns
3 bay leaves
4 sprigs fresh thyme

Salmon:
1 Norwegian Salmon fillet (2-3
   pounds), skinned and boned,
   cut in 4 ounce portions

Vinaigrette:
2 bunches watercress, washed
   and drained (divided)
4 ounces fresh chives, washed
   and drained (divided)
⅓ cup dill-flavored vinegar
1 tablespoon chopped parsley
2 tablespoons Dijon-style
   mustard
2 tablespoons fresh lemon
   juice
1 teaspoon sea salt
1 teaspoon white pepper
1 cup extra virgin olive oil
Lemon wedges—garnish

CAFE KNICKERBOCKER
1030 East Juneau Avenue
Milwaukee, Wisconsin

Refer to this recipe for a delicious, low calorie court bouillon for poaching fish and seafood. This beautiful recipe, from Chef Rob Wagner, could be adapted for use as an entree as well as an appetizer.

In a 5½ quart pan, place all ingredients for court bouillon. Bring to a boil over high heat; reduce heat and simmer for 20 minutes.

Place salmon portions in simmering court bouillon and poach 7-12 minutes or until salmon is opaque throughout. Remove salmon from court bouillon; drain on paper towel and refrigerate, covered, until time to assemble appetizer.

Make Watercress & Chive Vinaigrette by combining in work bowl of a food processor fitted with metal blade, 1 bunch of watercress leaves (stems discarded), half of chives (chopped), dill vinegar, chopped parsley, mustard, lemon juice, salt and white pepper. Process until smooth and blended, about 30 seconds.

Pour olive oil in a thin stream, slowly into vinaigrette while food processor is running until all oil is incorporated and vinaigrette forms a thick emulsion. Remove vinaigrette from processor and place in sealed bottle in refrigerator for 24-48 hours before using.

To assemble appetizer, drizzle vinaigrette on base of glass salad plate. Place a salmon portion on each plate and garnish with equal portions of remaining watercress leaves and chives. Garnish with lemon wedges.

BREADS AND BAKERY CHOICES

Lemon Bread

makes 1 large or 3 small loaves

1¼ cups sugar
½ cup vegetable oil
4 teaspoons grated lemon zest
2 teaspoons lemon extract
2 eggs, room temperature
2 cups flour
½ teaspoon salt
3½ teaspoons baking powder
¾ cup milk, room temperature

This lovely, lemony bread is a popular tradition at the White Gull Inn run by Jan and Andy Coulson. It is tasty with breakfast tea, excellent with a lunch salad and quite satisfying with dinner coffee. Bake it in three small loaves (5¾" x 3" loaf pans) for gift giving.

In a large mixing bowl with electric mixer, cream sugar, oil, lemon zest and lemon extract until blended. Beat in eggs, one at a time, beating after each addition. Set aside.

In a separate medium bowl, whisk together flour, salt and baking powder. Add dry ingredients to creamed mixture alternately with milk.

Grease one 8-inch x 4-inch loaf baking pan or three small pans as suggested above. Divide batter evenly between pans; batter will be pourable, not thick. Bake in preheated oven at 350°. Large loaf will take 60-65 minutes to bake; small loaves will bake in about 45 minutes. Check center of bread with clean wooden pick to determine if baked completely.

Remove from pans to cool on wire rack. Store in refrigerator wrapped in plastic wrap and aluminum foil.

THE WHITE GULL INN
4225 Main Street
Fish Creek, Wisconsin

Cherry Cream Cheese Bread

makes 1 loaf

Filling:

3 ounces cream cheese, softened
  (1 small package)
2 tablespoons sugar
1 tablespoon flour
1 egg yolk

Bread:

2 cups flour
½ cup brown sugar
1 tablespoon grated orange zest
1½ teaspoons baking powder
½ teaspoon salt
¼ cup unsalted butter
½ cup orange juice
1 extra large egg, beaten
2 cups fresh pitted tart cherries

This quick fruit bread from Pastry Chef Cheryl Poweleit is the most popular bread served at the Red Circle Inn. Its pretty red and creamy white interior and its excellent taste make this a great idea for holiday gift giving. Be sure to make some for your own family.

In a small bowl with electric mixer combine cream cheese, 2 tablespoons sugar, 1 tablespoon flour and egg yolk until smooth. Set aside.

Sift flour into a large bowl; add brown sugar, orange zest, baking powder and salt; combine. With a pastry blender, cut in butter until mixture resembles cornmeal. Stir in orange juice and beaten egg just until flour is moistened. Gently fold in cherries.

Spoon ⅔ of cherry batter mixture into a greased and floured 9″ x 5″ x 3″ loaf pan. Pour cream cheese mixture evenly over the batter. Spoon the remaining ⅓ batter over the top. Bake in a preheated 350° oven for 75 minutes or until a wooden pick inserted in center comes out clean. Cool in pan on wire rack for 10 minutes. Remove from pan and let cool completely. Refrigerate leftovers, tightly wrapped.

RED CIRCLE INN
N44 W33013 Watertown Plank Road
Nashotah, Wisconsin

Chocolate Zucchini Nut Bread

makes 1 loaf

3 large eggs
2 cups sugar
1 cup vegetable oil
1 teaspoon vanilla
2 cups grated zucchini (not
  peeled)
2 cups flour
1 teaspoon baking soda
1 teaspoon salt
1 teaspoon cinnamon
2 ounces unsweetened chocolate,
  melted
1 cup chopped nuts
⅔ cup semisweet chocolate chips

I've always had a theory about cookbooks. Namely, that one good new zucchini recipe could sell an entire cookbook. Here's a zucchini recipe from Pastry Chef Jeanne Demers that testers and families loved. See if you don't agree.

In a large mixing bowl, combine eggs, sugar, oil and vanilla until well blended, about 1½ minutes. Add zucchini and melted, cooled chocolate; stir to blend. Set aside.

Whisk together flour, baking soda, salt and cinnamon. Add dry ingredients, nuts and chocolate chips; stir only enough to blend in dry ingredients.

Spoon batter into a greased and floured 9" x 5" x 3" loaf pan. Bake in a preheated 350° oven for about 60-70 minutes or until a wooden pick inserted in center comes out clean. Cool in pan on wire rack for 10 minutes; turn out of pan and cool until just slightly warm to touch, about 1 hour. Wrap in plastic wrap; store in refrigerator.

THE INN AT CEDAR CROSSING
336 Louisiana Street
Sturgeon Bay, Wisconsin

Susie's Three Seed Bread

makes 2 loaves

1½ tablespoons active dry yeast
   or two packages ¼ ounce *each*
2 cups warm water (110-115°)
3 tablespoons brown sugar
¼ cup maple syrup
¼ cup olive oil
1 large egg, room temperature
5⅓ cups medium grind whole
   wheat flour
1⅔ cups unbleached flour
⅓ cup dry milk powder
1 tablespoon salt
1 tablespoon flax seed
1 tablespoon sesame seed
1 tablespoon amaranth seed

Pastry Chef Will Clark is known for his breads, especially this hearty and robust three-seeded yeast bread. The seeds for this bread are available at health food stores. This makes outstanding toast.

In a large mixing bowl, dissolve yeast in warm water; add brown sugar, maple syrup and olive oil. Beat in room temperature egg. Combine flours, powdered milk, salt, flax, sesame and amaranth seeds in separate bowl with whisk.

Stir half of dry ingredients together with yeast mixture (dough will be sticky). Add remaining dry ingredients stirring until incorporated. Cover with plastic wrap; let rise until double. *Don't let dough rise beyond double size—about 1 hour.* (Portion into 2 loaves—*each* 1 pound, 10 ounces.) Let rest for about 15 minutes.

Roll with rolling pin into 18-inch long by 6-inch wide rectangles. Roll up very tightly into cylinders, pressing out all air. Put into two greased 9″ x 5″ x 3″ loaf pans. Let rise until dough is ⅓ over top of pan. Bake in preheated 350° oven for 45 minutes. Turn out of pans onto cooling racks to cool completely.

SUSIE'S RESTAURANT
146 Fourth Avenue
Baraboo, Wisconsin

Olive Nut Rolls

makes 36 rolls

2 packages active dry yeast
  (¼ ounce *each*)
½ cup lukewarm water
  (110-115°)
½ cup unsalted butter
½ cup sugar
2 teaspoons salt
2 cups milk
7½ to 8 cups flour
1 cup chopped walnuts
¾ cup chopped stuffed green
  olives or pitted black olives
1 large egg, beaten slightly
1 tablespoon water

This is a recipe that Chef Nell Stehr varies by substituting freshly chopped herbs, shredded cheese, or bacon bits in place of the olives and nuts. It bakes up a lovely golden brown (see the rolls on the cover). Discover your own favorite variation.

In a small bowl, dissolve dry yeast in lukewarm water; set aside. In a small saucepan, combine butter, sugar, salt and milk. Heat over medium heat until butter melts. Cool until lukewarm.

In a large mixing bowl, add cooled milk mixture to the cooled yeast mixture. Gradually stir in flour until mixture forms a soft dough. Knead dough with bread hook until dough is smooth and elastic, 6-8 minutes.

Let dough rise in a well-greased, covered bowl until doubled in bulk, about 1½ hours. Punch dough down; flatten into a rectangle. Sprinkle surface with olives and walnuts; fold dough over and knead until walnuts and olives are incorporated in dough. Cut dough into 36 even pieces, roll each into a round ball and place in greased muffin tins or on a greased cookie sheet.

Let rise in a warm place, loosely covered, until doubled in bulk, about 40 minutes. Before baking, brush with an egg wash of beaten egg and 1 tablespoon water. Bake in a preheated 350° oven for 20 minutes or until nicely browned.

THE PAINTED LADY
518 Main Street
Newburg, Wisconsin

Blueberry Muffins

makes 24 large muffins

½ pound unsalted butter, room
    temperature
1½ cups sugar
6 large eggs
5 cups flour
2 teaspoons baking soda
1 teaspoon baking powder
¾ teaspoon salt
2½ cups dairy sour cream
3½ cups fresh or frozen
    blueberries

Tender, fruit-studded muffins with the richness of sour cream come through in these popular muffins from the Continental Cafe's Pastry Chef Lisa Ferguson. Make the full batch and freeze the extras for a homebaked treat on a hurried morning. Be advised that these are their popular oversized muffins so bake them in the largest tins you have.

In a large mixing bowl with electric mixer, cream butter and sugar together until light and fluffy, about 3 minutes. Add eggs, one at a time, beating well after each addition. Set aside.

Combine flour, baking soda, baking powder and salt and whisk together in a large bowl. Add half of dry ingredients into creamed mixture along with half of sour cream. Mix together until combined. Repeat with remaining half of dry ingredients and remaining half of sour cream; mix until combined. Do not overmix.

Fold in blueberries by hand using a spatula. Butter the muffin tins and surface area around tops of tins, or spray with vegetable oil spray. Spoon batter into 24 cups, filling each ¾ full. Bake in preheated 325° oven for about 30 minutes or until tops of muffins spring back when lightly touched. (Time will depend on size of muffin cups.) Remove muffins from pan to wire rack to cool or tilt each muffin on its side in pan to cool.

CONTINENTAL CAFE
19035 West Bluemound Road
Waukesha, Wisconsin

Chocolate Cherry Muffins

makes 12 muffins

2½ cups flour
1¾ cups sugar (divided)
10 tablespoons unsweetened cocoa
¾ teaspoon baking soda
2¼ teaspoons baking powder
1½ teaspoons salt
¾ cup unsalted butter
½ cups semisweet chocolate chips
2 cups pre-sweetened tart frozen cherries, thawed and well drained
2 large eggs
¾ cup milk (approximately)

Pastry Chef Jeanne Demers pulls out all the stops on this chocolate and cherry rich, yet not too sweet muffin. It could be dessert; it could be a snack. Or live on the edge—and have it for breakfast!

In a large mixing bowl combine flour, 1 cup of sugar, cocoa, baking soda, baking powder and salt with whisk. With a pastry blender, cut in butter until mixture resembles cornmeal. Add chocolate chips and well-drained cherries. Set aside.

Break eggs into a 2-cup measuring cup; add enough milk so the total amount of liquid ingredients measure 1¼ cups (this will depend on the size of the eggs). Whisk lightly to combine eggs and milk.

Stir into dry ingredients, mixing only until dry ingredients are combined. (Batter will be stiff.) Grease the top edges of each cup of a 12-cup muffin tin, lining each cup with paper liners. Fill liners until batter is slightly mounded over top. Sprinkle each top with about 1 tablespoon sugar from remaining ¾ cup granulated sugar.

Bake in a preheated 350° oven for about 25 minutes or until wooden pick inserted in center of muffin comes out clean. Remove from muffin tin to cool on wire rack.

THE INN AT CEDAR CROSSING
336 Louisiana Street
Sturgeon Bay, Wisconsin

Bacon Cheddar Biscuits

makes 12 biscuits

2 cups flour
4 teaspoons baking powder
½ teaspoon salt
¼ teaspoon black pepper
½ cup shortening
⅔ cup milk, room temperature
¼ cup minced onion
½ cup crisply fried bacon bits (8 strips)
½ cup shredded sharp Cheddar cheese

Chef Amy Crowns adds a bit of down-home taste to her uptown biscuits. Jim and Ellen Jensen, owners of The Vintage, recommend these as a fine brunch or supper fare.

In a medium mixing bowl, whisk together flour, baking powder, salt and pepper. Cut in shortening with pastry blender until mixture resembles cornmeal.

Add milk, stir in onion, bacon and cheese until dough just clings together. Do not overmix.

Drop rounded tablespoons of dough on greased cookie sheet, 2 inches apart. Bake in preheated 450° oven for about 10 minutes or until golden brown.

THE VINTAGE
3110 8th Street South
Wisconsin Rapids, Wisconsin

Almond Tea Cakes

makes 36 mini tea cakes

2½ cups flour
½ teaspoon salt
2 teaspoons baking powder
2 cups sugar
4 large eggs
1 cup vegetable oil
½ cup white wine
½ cup apple juice
1 teaspoon almond extract
1 teaspoon vanilla extract
½ cup sliced almonds
Sliced almonds—garnish

Not too sweet yet these tender little almond-stuffed cakes are just the right thing to serve with tea or coffee when you want something fancier than a muffin or scone. Our thanks to Executive Chef James Simmers for sharing his recipe.

Sift flour, salt and baking powder together; set aside. In a large mixing bowl with electric mixer, combine sugar and eggs. Beat at medium speed for 1 minute.

Add vegetable oil, wine, juice, almond and vanilla extracts and continue beating at medium speed for 1 minute more. Fold in flour mixture and almonds, taking care not to overmix batter.

Spoon batter into greased miniature muffin tins, ¾ full. Top lightly with additional sliced almonds. Bake in preheated 375° oven for 17-20 minutes or until golden brown. Cool in tins on wire rack. Remove from tins; store in covered container.

CARVERS ON THE LAKE
RESTAURANT AND INN
N5529 County Trunk A
Green Lake, Wisconsin

Jesse's
Almond Buttermilk Scones

makes 12 scones

3 cups flour
½ cup sugar
½ cup sliced almonds
2¾ teaspoons baking powder
½ teaspoon salt
2 tablespoons cold unsalted
   butter, cut into small pieces
2 large eggs
¾ cup buttermilk, room
   temperature
½ teaspoon almond extract

Perfect for tea, lovely at a wedding shower and a real treat for brunch, these delicately almond scented-and-studded scones should become a part of your quick bread file. Shape them with heart-shaped cutters for a romantic touch.

In a large mixing bowl, combine flour, sugar, almonds, baking powder and salt. Cut in butter with pastry blender until mixture is crumbly—the size of tiny peas. Combine eggs, buttermilk and almond extract; stir into flour mixture until just combined.

Turn onto floured surface; press gently into a round 1½ inches thick. *Do not overwork.* Cut into 2-inch rounds with fluted biscuit cutter; place on greased baking sheet in preheated 350° about 20 minutes. Serve warm.

THE OVENS OF BRITTANY
305 State Street
Madison, Wisconsin

Corn Fritters

makes 20 fritters

2 cups flour, sifted
1 teaspoon salt
2 tablespoons baking powder
1 tablespoon corn oil
1½ teaspoons vinegar
1 cup milk
3 large eggs, separated
1 cup niblet canned corn,
    drained
Vegetable shortening for deep
    frying

Fritters are popular—just read through the various fritter offerings of our chefs. This is an American classic and proudly served at Boder's down through the years. Their recipe and methods are time tested and delicious.

Sift flour, salt and baking powder together in medium bowl. Add oil, vinegar, milk, egg yolks and corn. Mix well—mixture should be moist, not dry. Set aside.

In a small deep non-plastic mixing bowl, beat egg whites on high speed until stiff, not dry, about 2 minutes. Gently fold egg whites into batter. Set aside.

Heat shortening in deep skillet or electric frying pan to 350°. Drop rounded tablespoon of batter carefully into hot fat. Deep-fry about 4 minutes until golden brown (fritters will turn over by themselves). Remove from oil; drain quickly on paper towel and place finished fritter in empty muffin tin; bake in preheated 325° oven for 10 minutes. Sprinkle with powdered sugar and serve warm with maple syrup.

BODER'S ON THE RIVER
11919 North River Road
Mequon, Wisconsin

Creole Cheese Fritters
with Dijon Sauce

makes 18 fritters

Fritters:

1 cup flour
½ cup yellow cornmeal
1 teaspoon baking powder
1 teaspoon salt
2 large eggs
½ cup milk, room temperature
½ cup sharp Cheddar cheese,
    shredded
1 teaspoon fresh* or canned
    jalapeno peppers, minced
¼ cup minced red bell pepper
Vegetable oil for deep-frying

Sauce:

1 cup mayonnaise
2 tablespoons Dijon-style
    mustard
1 tablespoon Worcestershire
    sauce

Hot peppers and sweet red bell peppers add color and flavor to these fritters with a Creole heritage from Chef Amy Crowns.

In a large mixing bowl, whisk together flour, cornmeal, baking powder and salt. Stir in eggs and milk, mixing to blend. Fold in cheese, jalapeno and red bell pepper just enough to incorporate.

Heat oil for deep-frying until temperature reaches 350°. Carefully drop by rounded tablespoons into hot oil and fry for about 2 minutes on each side or until completely done. (If fritters do not turn by themselves part way through frying, gently turn them over to complete frying.)

Drain completely on several layers of paper towel. Serve warm with sauce that is made by combining all sauce ingredients until blended. This makes a good side dish and can serve as an appetizer with the addition of chopped clams, crab or shrimp added to the batter.

* *Use kitchen gloves when handling fresh peppers. Avoid contact with eyes. Wash hands with soap and cold water after handling.*

THE VINTAGE
3110 8th Street South
Wisconsin Rapids, Wisconsin

Dried Cherry Fritters

makes 20 fritters

1¼ cups flour
1 tablespoon baking soda
2 tablespoons sugar
½ teaspoon salt
½ teaspoon ground allspice
2 large eggs
1 cup cultured buttermilk
1 tablespoon unsalted butter,
  melted
1 cup dried cherries
Vegetable shortening or oil for
  frying
Cinnamon sugar

Dried cherries are one of the more recent products to come out of Door County and if you haven't tried them, please do. Here's a grand fritter recipe from Master Chef Craig Kuenning that uses dried cherries with a spark of allspice in the batter.

In a small mixing bowl combine flour, baking soda, sugar, salt and allspice with wire whisk. Set aside.

In a medium bowl with electric mixer, beat eggs and buttermilk together. Add cherries and melted butter to egg mixture. Stir in dry ingredients all at once with wooden spoon. Stir just enough to moisten.

Drop by tablespoons into fat which has been heated to 350°. Fry for 5 minutes, turning fritters with fork after 2½ minutes if they do not turn over by themselves. Remove to paper towels and drain. While still hot, dredge in a mixture of sugar and cinnamon.

QUIVEY'S GROVE
6261 Nesbitt Road
Madison, Wisconsin

SOUPS

Chilled Plum Soup

makes 4 servings

1½ cups pitted, chopped dark
  plums
½ cup apple juice
¾ cup dry white wine (divided)
¼ teaspoon ground cinnamon
⅛ teaspoon ground cloves
⅛ teaspoon ground ginger
½ cup sugar or to taste
1 tablespoon fresh squeezed
  lemon juice, strained
½ cup heavy whipping cream

This beautiful soup, the color of rasp-berry sherbet, has just the right amount of piquant/sweet flavors, so pretty that we put it on the cover. Make this soup in advance, refrigerate, and serve in dainty small servings for special occasion dinners.

In a heavy medium-size saucepan, combine plums, apple juice, ½ cup wine, cinnamon, cloves and ginger. Bring to a boil, covered, over medium/high heat and boil gently until soft and fork tender, about 15 minutes, stirring occasionally.

Strain through a sieve; discard plum pulp. Add sugar to plum juice and refrigerate until cool, about 2 hours. May refrigerate overnight.

When cool, whisk in remaining ¼ cup wine, lemon juice and whipping cream. Serve in a chilled cup with chilled bouillon spoon.

THE BOULEVARD INN
925 East Wells Street
Milwaukee, Wisconsin

Acorn Squash Soup
with Curried Apples
makes 6-8 servings

2 large acorn squash (about 6
   pounds), seeds removed and
   cut in quarters
4 baking apples, peeled and
   cored
⅓ cup brandy
1 tablespoon curry powder
1 teaspoon nutmeg
1 teaspoon cinnamon
8 cups chicken stock
2 cups heavy whipping cream
8 baked apple slices—garnish

A perfect pureed soup for fall that combines squash, apples and spices. This would be a fine starter for a Thanksgiving feast—our thanks to Chef Peter Baldus.

Place quartered squash and prepared apples in a baking dish and bake in preheated 350° oven for 30 minutes or until both are tender. When squash is cool enough to handle, remove the squash meat from the skins; discarding skins. In a food processor bowl fitted with a metal blade, puree the squash and apple together until smooth, about 1 minute.

Pour the brandy in a 5-quart kettle, ignite the brandy with a flame and cook over medium heat until the flame dies. Add the squash puree, curry powder, nutmeg, cinnamon and chicken stock. Cook until mixture is reduced by two-thirds, about 45 minutes.

Add cream and bring mixture to a simmer over medium heat. To serve soup, garnish with a baked apple slice sprinkled with additional curry or serve in an acorn squash shell which has been baked and scraped out leaving ½-inch of squash meat to support the skin. This may be made ahead, refrigerated and gently reheated.

RED CIRCLE INN
N44 W33013 Watertown Plank Road
Nashotah, Wisconsin

Cream of Mushroom Soup

makes 8 servings

1 pound mushrooms, cleaned,
  trimmed and chopped
½ cup chopped onions
2 quarts chicken broth
½ cup unsalted butter, melted
½ cup flour
1 cup heavy whipping cream
1-2 tablespoons fresh lemon
  juice
Sour cream—garnish
Sprig of watercress or
  parsley—garnish

If you have never made a homemade Cream of Mushroom Soup, you should try this delightfully seasoned version from Chef Nell Stehr. Smooth and tasty, it will please cream soup lovers everywhere.

In a large kettle, combine chopped mushrooms, onion and chicken broth. Cook over medium heat until mushrooms are tender, about 10 minutes. Strain off the broth, reserving both mushrooms and broth. Set aside.

In a 2-quart saucepan, make a roux by melting butter until bubbly over medium heat; whisk in flour gradually. Cook, stirring constantly for 2 minutes. Whisk in reserved liquid, adding gradually. Bring mixture to a boil.

Add reserved mushrooms and cream. Heat *just to the boiling point. Do not boil.* Whisk in lemon juice. Serve in warm soup cups. Garnish with a dollop of sour cream and a sprig of watercress or parsley.

THE PAINTED LADY
518 Main Street
Newburg, Wisconsin

Creamy Onion and Garlic Soup

makes 2½ quarts

½ cup unsalted butter
1½ cups diced onions
1 tablespoon minced garlic
⅛ teaspoon nutmeg
½ cup flour
6 cups chicken stock
¼ cup sherry
2 cups heavy whipping cream
Dash of white pepper
Dash of cayenne
Dash of onion powder

A delicately flavored cream-based first course that prepares the palette for delights to follow. All soups are popular at Jacobi's of Hazelhurst but this is the most requested of all their soup offerings. Don't hesitate on the nutmeg. It imparts just the right flavor—a wonderful soup from Alan and Pam Jacobi.

In a 3½-quart heavy-bottomed kettle, melt butter over low heat. Add onions, garlic and nutmeg; cook until onions are tender, about 6 minutes.

Whisk in flour, cook over low heat for 3 minutes. *Do not brown.* Gradually stir in chicken stock and sherry. Bring to a boil over medium/high heat. Boil for 5 minutes. Reduce heat to low. Whisk in cream. Correct seasoning with white pepper, cayenne, onion powder, and additional nutmeg, if desired.

JACOBI'S OF HAZELHURST
9820 Cedar Falls Road
Hazelhurst, Wisconsin

Bavarian Lentil Soup

makes twelve 4-ounce servings

16 ounces dried lentils
3 quarts beef or chicken stock
7 ounces bacon, diced
4 ounces ham, diced
1 cup diced carrot
1 cup diced onion
1 cup diced celery
2 teaspoons salt
1 teaspoon freshly ground black
    pepper
1½ cups red wine vinegar or to
    taste
1 cup brown sugar
1 bay leaf

A lighter than usual legume soup that skillfully blends sweet/sour flavors in a slightly smoky flavored broth base. A delicious soup created by Chef Knut F. Apitz.

In a 5 or 6-quart stockpot, soak lentils and water (2 parts water to 1 part lentils) overnight. Drain off excess water and add stock to lentils. Heat over medium/high heat while other ingredients are being prepared.

In a 9-inch diameter skillet fry diced bacon until crisp over medium/high heat (5 minutes) and add bacon bits to soup, reserving bacon fat to sauté ham, carrot, onion and celery for 1-2 minutes. Add vegetables and ham to soup.

Simmer soup, covered over medium/low heat until lentils are tender, about 1 hour. Remove bay leaf.

GRENADIER'S RESTAURANT
747 North Broadway at Mason
Milwaukee, Wisconsin

Reuben Soup

makes 8 servings

½ cup unsalted butter plus 1
   tablespoon (divided)
1 cup diced onion
4 cups water
1 cup sauerkraut, not rinsed,
   coarsely chopped
2 cups cooked corn beef,
   coarsely chopped
¼ cup powdered chicken soup
   base
2 teaspoons Dijon-style mustard
¼ teaspoon horseradish
1 teaspoon dried dill weed
¼ teaspoon freshly ground black
   pepper
1 teaspoon sugar
½ cup flour
4 cups scalded milk (heated to
   180°F.)
2 cups shredded Swiss cheese
Freshly minced
   parsley—garnish

A perfect après ski soup that uses all those yummy flavors of a Reuben Sandwich and if possible, even makes them better. This is a crowd pleaser. (Great for leftovers from Reuben Sandwiches.)

Melt 1 tablespoon butter in a heavy 4-quart saucepan. Add onions and sauté over medium/high heat until onions are browned, about 2-3 minutes. Add water, sauerkraut, beef, chicken base, mustard, horseradish, dill, pepper and sugar. Bring to a boil; reduce heat and simmer over low heat for 5 minutes.

Make a roux from ½ cup remaining butter by melting butter in a heavy 2-quart saucepan and whisking in flour. Cook, stirring constantly over low heat for 5 minutes.

Whisk in hot milk and cheese, blending well. Stir roux mixture into soup base, blending well. Pour into soup bowls and garnish with parsley. Serve with dark rye bread.

THE KITCHEN TABLE
East 3rd and Maple
Marshfield, Wisconsin

Thai Chicken Soup - Grill Style

makes 9 servings

Marinade:

¼ cup dark or roasted sesame
  oil, oriental-style
1½ tablespoons minced fresh
  mint
2 tablespoons minced fresh
  cilantro
1 teaspoon grated fresh ginger
¾ teaspoon minced seeded fresh
  jalapeno pepper
3 cloves minced garlic
2 tablespoons minced fresh basil

Vegetables:

5 ounces untrimmed shiitake
  mushrooms, trimmed, cleaned,
  sliced
6 small green onions, minced
⅓ cup julienne red bell pepper,
  large matchstick cut
⅓ cup julienne green bell pepper,
  large matchstick cut
1 cup peeled julienne carrot,
  large matchstick cut

Chicken Soup:

1 whole chicken breast (8
  ounces), skinned and boned
10 cups chicken stock
4 ounces rice sticks, broken in 2-
  inch lengths
1 teaspoon fresh lime juice
1 tablespoon balsamic vinegar
1 teaspoon Hoisin sauce (or to
  taste)*
Salt to taste
Freshly ground black pepper to
  taste

*If you like Thai food and something
that stretches your soup repertoire imag-
inatively, take a bit of time and make
this wonderful, complexly-flavored
soup created by Chefs Christy and
Craig. Rich in colorful vegetables and
unique flavors, this is a fun recipe. You
can easily find rice sticks in the Oriental
sections of supermarkets.*

WILSON STREET GRILL
217 South Hamilton
Madison, Wisconsin

Combine marinade ingredients together in a small mixing bowl. Set aside. Place prepared mushrooms, green onions, red and green peppers and carrots in medium mixing bowl; add half of marinade. Toss to coat vegetables and marinate, covered, in refrigerator for 2-3 hours or overnight.

Pour remaining marinade over chicken breast in plastic self-sealing bag. Refrigerate for at least 2-3 hours. Drain chicken, discarding marinade. Grill over hot grill, turning once, cooking each side about 4 minutes depending on thickness of chicken. Remove to cutting surface, tear apart into strands. Set aside.

Bring chicken stock to a boil in a 4-quart kettle. Add drained marinated vegetables; simmer 15 minutes or until tender/crisp. Presoak rice sticks for 10 minutes in water; drain. Add rice sticks to broth; cook for 15 minutes or until tender. Add chicken pieces and correct seasoning by adding lime juice, vinegar, Hoisin sauce (taste as you go*) and salt and pepper, if desired.

Sun Prairie Corn Chowder

makes 8 servings

4 ounces bacon, cut into ¼-inch
   strips
1 medium onion, diced, about ½
   cup
1 sweet red bell pepper, diced,
   about ¾ cup
4 tablespoons flour
1 quart chicken stock
2 baking potatoes, diced, about
   1½ cups
4 cups sweet corn, fresh or
   frozen
1 cup finely diced ham
1 cup heavy whipping cream
Salt to taste
¼ teaspoon freshly ground black
   pepper

Chef Scott McGlinchey included these delightful comments with his Corn Chowder recipe. "In late summer, Sun Prairie is my favorite place to go for corn. The Sun Prairie Corn Fest is always so much fun, eating ear after ear of fresh roasted corn rolled in fine Wisconsin butter and salting it off of the hundreds of salt shakers that adorn the grounds. We always freeze up plenty for the whole year to make this favorite corn chowder at the restaurant."

In a heavy-bottomed 5-quart kettle, sauté the bacon over medium/high heat until almost crisp, about 3 minutes. Add the onion and pepper to skillet and cook, stirring occasionally, until onions are translucent, about 1 minute.

Whisk in the flour and cook over low heat, stirring constantly for 3-4 minutes. Gradually whisk in the chicken stock, whisking to blend ingredients. Add potatoes and corn. Bring mixture to a boil over high heat; cover and reduce heat. Simmer until potatoes are tender, about 15 minutes.

Add the ham, cream, salt to taste and pepper and heat thoroughly. Serve hot.

HEAVEN CITY RESTAURANT
*S91 W27850 National Avenue
Mukwonago, Wisconsin*

Whitefish Chowder

makes 8 large servings

1½ pounds of whitefish fillets
2 cups water
1 teaspoon salt
2 cups peeled diced potatoes
½ cup diced carrots
1 cup diced onion
½ cup diced green bell pepper
½ cup diced red bell pepper
2 teaspoons hot pepper sauce
2 teaspoons Angostura bitters
¼ teaspoon freshly ground black
   pepper
1 teaspoon garlic powder
1 tablespoon fresh lemon juice
24 ounces clam juice
4 cups milk
½ cup bacon fat
½ cup flour

I tasted this colorful, hearty chowder on my way home from a winter weekend in Door County. It was definitely love at first spoonful. The Cookery is understandably proud of this popular creation, and we are so pleased that they would share it.

In a large 6-quart kettle or stockpot, place water and whitefish. Bring to a boil over medium high heat. Reduce heat and simmer, covered, 15 minutes or until fish flakes easily with a fork. Remove fish from broth and set aside.

Add salt, potatoes, carrots, onions and green and red pepper to fish broth. Boil, covered, about 10 minutes or until potatoes and carrots are tender/crisp.

Add hot pepper sauce, bitters, black pepper, garlic powder, lemon juice, clam juice and milk. Bring to a boil; reduce heat and let simmer while making a roux.

In a heavy medium saucepan, heat bacon drippings until completely melted and gradually whisk in flour. Let cook over medium heat, whisking constantly for one minute. Slowly whisk roux into simmering chowder.

Gently stir in reserved fish; blend with other ingredients. Serve hot.

THE COOKERY
4135 Main Street, Hwy. 42
Fish Creek, Wisconsin

Wild Rice and Mushroom Broth

makes 8 servings

½ pound wild rice, rinsed and
   drained
9 cups water
4 tablespoons unsalted butter
   (divided)
1 ounce dried cepes (porcini)
   mushrooms
1 pound button mushrooms,
   coarsely chopped
1 clove garlic, coarsely chopped
8 large shallots, coarsely
   chopped
1 teaspoon salt
½ teaspoon white pepper
2 cups good quality medium
   sherry
4 tablespoons fresh chopped
   thyme
1 bay leaf
2-inch stem of fresh rosemary
½ pound shiitake mushrooms,
   stems removed

An absolutely stunning first course from Odessa Piper that utilizes the woodsy flavor of wild mushrooms and the textural beauty of wild rice in a sherry-laced broth that is both light and rich.

In a 3½ to 4 quart saucepan, boil rice and water together over medium heat, covered, until tender, about 40 minutes. Drain, reserving rice water and rice. Set aside.

Melt 3 tablespoons butter in large heavy-bottomed 12-inch diameter sauté pan over medium heat. Add cepes, button mushrooms, garlic, shallots, salt and pepper, stirring occasionally until juices are rendered from mushrooms. Increase heat to high, take off heat and add sherry.

Return to heat. (You may ignite sherry if desired.) Reduce this liquid mash by half and add reserved rice water, thyme, bay leaf and rosemary.

Simmer on low heat for 30 minutes. Strain through fine chinoise or triple layer cheese cloth.

Add 2 cups of pre-cooked wild rice to broth. Cut shiitake mushrooms in ¼-inch pieces. In a 9-inch diameter skillet sauté shiitake mushrooms in remaining 1 tablespoon butter for about 2 minutes. Add to broth. Adjust seasoning.

L'ETOILE
25 North Pinckney
Madison, Wisconsin

SALADS AND SALAD DRESSINGS

Creamy House Dressing

makes 1 quart

¾ cup dairy sour cream
¾ cup nonfat plain yogurt
1 cup reduced calorie
  mayonnaise
⅔ cup freshly grated Parmesan
  cheese
1 cup cultured buttermilk
¾ teaspoon garlic powder
¾ teaspoon onion powder
1½ teaspoons cracked (coarsely
  ground) black pepper
1½ teaspoons fresh lemon juice
1½ teaspoons paprika

A popular reduced calorie and fat dressing favored by many patrons at Sweetwaters. It keeps well, refrigerated and covered and goes nicely with a variety of salad greens.

Combine all ingredients in blender, or work bowl of food processor, or in a mixing bowl with electric mixer and mix until smooth, about 1 minute. Store in a covered glass container in refrigerator. This will keep for 4 weeks, refrigerated.

SWEETWATERS
1104 West Clairemont Avenue
Eau Claire, Wisconsin

Pecan Garlic Dressing

makes 1¼ cups

¼ cup red wine vinegar
3 teaspoons minced fresh garlic
½ teaspoon salt
¼ teaspoon freshly ground black
   pepper
½ teaspoon sugar
¾ cup olive oil
¼ cup coarsely chopped toasted
   or untoasted pecans

We weren't certain that Chef Benny Smith would part with his tasty Pecan Garlic Salad Dressing recipe. He did; and we are grateful. The pecans, which he says may be toasted or not, add a special taste and textural richness. We liked the pecans toasted.

In a small mixing bowl, combine vinegar, minced garlic, salt, black pepper, and sugar. Whisk together until salt and sugar are dissolved. Slowly whisk in olive oil, pouring oil in a thin stream. Stir in pecans. Do not refrigerate dressing.

BENNY'S KITCHEN
239 West Main Street
Waukesha, Wisconsin

Door County Cherry Vinaigrette

makes 3¼ cups

Vinegar:

1 pint tart, red cherries*
2 cups white wine vinegar

Vinaigrette:

2 cups vegetable oil
1 cup cherry vinegar
6 tablespoons fresh lemon juice
1½ teaspoons celery salt
1½ teaspoons sugar or to taste
1½ teaspoons Dijon-style
  mustard
¾ teaspoon paprika
¾ teaspoon white pepper
1 teaspoon Worcestershire sauce

The White Apron, like so many Door County inns and restaurants, does an excellent job of promoting Door County foods. Here's a pretty, slightly piquant dressing from Chef Barbara McCarrier that showcases cherries from the pennisula.

To make cherry vinegar, place cherries in a glass or stainless steel container with a minimum of 2-quart capacity. Cover with vinegar; stir gently. Let stand, covered for 48 hours at room temperature. Drain liquid off cherries for use in vinaigrette. Use cherries for garnish on salad.

Combine oil, cherry vinegar, lemon juice, celery salt, sugar, Dijon-style mustard, paprika, white pepper and Worcestershire sauce in blender, work bowl of food processor or in a bowl with electric mixer. Blend for 30 seconds. Store in covered glass container in refrigerator. Use on a salad of mixed greens.

* *You may use frozen, drained cherries or canned (no sugar added) cherries.*

THE WHITE APRON
414 Maple Drive
Sister Bay, Wisconsin

Mixed Greens Salad

makes 4 servings

Salad Mix:

Red and green Bibb lettuce
Red and green Loose-leaf
  lettuce
Red and green Romaine
  lettuce
Swiss Chard
Chicory
Radicchio
Red Russian Kale
Spinach
Lovage
Variety of herbs

Chef Barbara McCarrier orders her mixed greens for this salad from Bright Eye Farm, an organic market in Sturgeon Bay. For your convenience she includes a partial list of edible greens that may be used in this tasty salad mix that she serves with Cherry Vinaigrette Dressing. Check your grocery store's produce departments for specialty salad mixed greens. It may sometimes be sold as Mesclun—a mixture of tiny greens.

Wash, drain and thoroughly chill 8 cups of torn, mixed greens. Divide evenly between 4 chilled glass salad plates. Drizzle with Cherry Vinaigrette and top with reserved cherries.

THE WHITE APRON
414 Maple Drive
Sister Bay, Wisconsin

Hearts of Artichoke and Peapod Salad

makes 6 servings

6 hearts of artichokes, canned or
   fresh
4 ounces fresh pea pods
4 ounces fresh mushrooms,
   washed
1 teaspoon minced fresh garlic
1 teaspoon dried dill weed
1 teaspoon salt
1 teaspoon freshly ground black
   pepper
2 teaspoons Dijon-style mustard
¼ cup red wine vinegar
¼ cup vegetable oil
1 cup half-and-half
2 ounces toasted sliced almonds

An unusual salad from Chef Knut F. Apitz that offers a delicious alternative to the customary mixed greens offerings. A light, creamy dill dressing binds this all together in an exceptionally tasty salad course.

Cut artichoke hearts in half lengthwise; dry on paper towels. Cut the pea pods in ½-inch pieces. Slice the mushrooms ⅛-inch thick. Set all vegetables aside in a large mixing bowl.

In a medium bowl, make dressing by whisking together garlic, dill weed, salt, pepper, mustard, vinegar and oil until well-combined. Slowly stir in half-and-half to blend.

Pour enough dressing over vegetables to coat to your pleasure. Toss gently; sprinkle with almonds.

GRENADIER'S RESTAURANT
*747 North Broadway at Mason
Milwaukee, Wisconsin*

Asparagus Salad
with Lemon Dijon Dressing
makes 4 servings

Dressing:

5 tablespoons fresh lemon juice
2 tablespoons Dijon-style
 mustard
2 tablespoons sugar
1 teaspoon salt
1 teaspoon freshly ground black
 pepper
1 clove garlic, crushed, about 1
 teaspoon
1 cup vegetable oil

Salad:

1 pound fresh asparagus
1 head red leaf lettuce
2 hard-cooked eggs, peeled and
 coarsely chopped

QUIVEY'S GROVE
6261 Nesbitt Road
Madison, Wisconsin

If you think that asparagus and lemon were made for each other, do make this pretty luncheon salad from Master Chef Craig Kuenning. Most of the work can be done ahead and all the cook needs is a few minutes for final arrangement and garnishes.

Combine all dressing ingredients except oil in blender or bowl with wire whisk. Slowly whisk in vegetable oil in thin stream, whisking until dressing is thick and all oil is incorporated. Set aside.

Break off tough ends of asparagus. Blanch in 9-inch diameter skillet in boiling water to cover until just tender/crisp, about 2-3 minutes. Immediately plunge asparagus into ice water to stop cooking. Drain on paper towels.

Cut off asparagus tips; reserve for garnish. Cut remainder into ¾-inch pieces; marinate in 1 cup dressing for at least 2 hours.

Wash lettuce thoroughly; discard any damaged leaves. Drain well on paper towels, chill thoroughly. Reserve 12 of the best leaves to use in lining 4 salad plates; tear up remainder of lettuce and toss with some of the dressing.

Line 4 salad plates, each with 3 leaves. Divide torn lettuce with dressing between plates. Drain dressing from remaining asparagus and divide evenly between plates, mounding in center. Sprinkle each plate with ¼ of chopped egg. Garnish with asparagus tips.

Carrot Salad
with Cider Dressing
makes 15 cups

Carrot Salad:

3 pounds carrots, peeled, sliced in ½ lengthwise, then diagonally in 1-inch pieces

1½ green bell peppers, sliced in ¼-inch thick lengthwise strips

1 medium white onion, sliced in ¼-inch thick rings

Cider Dressing:

1 cup ketchup
½ cup sugar
⅓ cup apple cider vinegar
⅓ cup olive oil
1½ teaspoons freshly ground black pepper
1 tablespoon dry mustard
1½ tablespoons cornstarch

Susie Quiriconi, owner of Susie's Restaurant got this salad from Sue Adix of the Kitchen Hearth, a gourmet take-out shop in Madison on Mineral Point Road. "When I started Susie's I told Sue Adix that I wanted something besides French Fries to serve on the side of my sandwiches. Since I was always buying her Carrot Salad, I offered to buy the recipe. She told me she would give me the recipe (her grandmother's) for my use at the restaurant. In this same spirit I share the recipe with patrons and now with your readers."

In a large saucepan, combine carrots and about 3½ cups of water to nearly cover carrots. Bring to a boil; reduce heat and simmer until tender-crisp, about 10-12 minutes. Drain water from carrots; set aside.

In a medium saucepan, combine ketchup, sugar, vinegar, olive oil, pepper, mustard and cornstarch whisking together until smooth. Bring to a boil; boil 1 minute. Remove from heat. Add sliced green peppers and onions to carrots; pour hot dressing over vegetable mixture. Refrigerate, covered. This will keep, refrigerated, for up to 1 week.

SUSIE'S RESTAURANT
146 Fourth Avenue
Baraboo, Wisconsin

Spinach Salad
with Hazelnut Vinaigrette
makes 4 servings

Vinaigrette:
⅓ cup fresh lemon juice, strained
⅓ cup balsamic vinegar
¼ cup Dijon-style mustard
3 tablespoons honey
1 tablespoon Worcestershire
　sauce
¼ teaspoon salt
¼ teaspoon freshly ground black
　pepper
¼ cup finely chopped hazelnuts
10 tablespoons hazelnut oil or
　olive oil

Salad:
1 pound fresh spinach leaves,
　stemmed, washed, drained,
　chilled
4 strips lean bacon, fried until
　crisp, crumbled
½ cup coarsely chopped
　hazelnuts
1 can (11 ounces) mandarin
　oranges, drained
4 ounces fresh button
　mushrooms, cleaned, trimmed,
　sliced

This pretty salad from Executive Chef Scott Maanum with its interesting components is substantial enough to make a satisfying lunch or light supper. Serve it with a whole grain roll, if you like.

In a medium bowl, whisk together lemon juice, vinegar, mustard, honey, Worcestershire sauce, salt, pepper and finely chopped hazelnuts. Slowly beat in oil in a fine stream until all oil is incorporated. Set aside.

Divide spinach between four chilled salad plates. Top plates with one-fourth *each* of bacon, coarsely chopped hazelnuts, oranges and mushrooms. Drizzle each salad with one-fourth of Hazelnut Vinaigrette. Garnish with mushrooms and oranges, if desired.

**STOUT'S LODGE
ISLAND OF HAPPY DAYS**
*Red Cedar Lake
Mikana, Wisconsin*

Ensalada De Nopales
(Cactus Salad)

Salad:

2½ pounds fresh cactus leaves
1 red onion, diced
¼ large jicama, about 1 cup,
   cut in julienne
1 red bell pepper, diced
1 Poblano pepper, diced

Vinaigrette:

6 tablespoons vinegar
½ cup olive oil
1 teaspoon freshly ground
   black pepper
1½ teaspoons salt
½ teaspoon leaf oregano,
   crumbled
1½ teaspoons Worcestershire
   sauce

The next time you serve Mexican or southwest food, do try this delightful marinated cactus salad. The taste of cactus will remind you of roasted peppers and is therefore delightfully pleasant. You will find fresh cactus leaves in Hispanic markets or in produce departments of large supermarkets.

Carefully trim edges and spikes off of cactus leaves. Cut in ¼-inch wide strips. Heat large kettle with 4 cups of salted water and bring to a boil. Add cactus strips. Boil 10-15 minutes, uncovered; drain thoroughly. Chill cactus strips.

Whisk together salad dressing ingredients in small bowl. Pour over chilled cactus, onion, jicama, peppers. Cover and chill for 2 hours.

CLUB CHA CHA
1332 West Lincoln Avenue
Milwaukee, Wisconsin

PASTA, SIDE DISHES AND VEGETARIAN CHOICES

Breadcrumb Salsa

makes 6 cups

1 cup extra virgin olive oil
   (divided)
½ cup minced red bell pepper
½ cup minced yellow bell pepper
½ cup minced red onion
6 cups soft bread crumbs (from
   good-quality French bread)
1 teaspoon salt
½ cup minced fresh parsley
1 cup diced fresh tomatoes

Bread stuffing fans who don't wish to feel guilty about how much they love the stuff, might want to try this pretty accompaniment to any cooked or grilled fish. This innovation from Christy and Craig has plate appeal.

In a 9-inch diameter skillet or sauté pan over medium/high heat, sauté in ½ cup olive oil, red and yellow pepper and onion until soft but not brown, about 2 minutes. Add bread crumbs and salt to taste.

Stir constantly until bread crumbs just begin to get golden from heat. Add remaining ½ cup olive oil, parsley and tomatoes; heat through and serve warm with catfish or other fish like MahiMahi.

WILSON STREET GRILL
217 South Hamilton
Madison, Wisconsin

Green Onion and Garlic Bread Pudding

makes 4 servings

1 cup heavy whipping cream
1 large egg
1 egg yolk
¼ teaspoon salt
1 tablespoon fresh minced garlic
3 green onions, finely sliced
  (divided)
2 cups sour dough bread cubes,
  cut ¼-inch in size

The test staff loved these golden brown soufflelike side dishes that would be wonderful served with Prime Rib or any good beef roast. The base ingredients can be mixed together several hours before serving, covered and refrigerated until baking time. Do try these puddings from Master Chef Craig Kuenning.

Combine cream, egg, yolk, salt, garlic and half of onions in small mixing bowl. Cover and refrigerate for 2 hours.

Spray four 6-ounce custard cups with vegetable spray. Place ½ cup of bread cubes in each and pour one-fourth of egg mixture over each. Push remaining green onions into top of each cup.

Bake in a preheated 350° oven for about 35 minutes or until set and brown on top. Remove from oven; let set in warm place for 15 minutes. Run a knife around cup edge and turn out onto serving plates. Quivey's Grove serves these with Prime Rib.

QUIVEY'S GROVE
6261 Nesbitt Road
Madison, Wisconsin

Colcannon

makes 6-8 servings

4 large potatoes, peeled and
   diced, about 4 cups
1 cup heavy whipping cream
½ teaspoon chopped garlic
1 teaspoon dried parsley flakes
1 teaspoon salt
½ teaspoon white pepper
1 cup chopped green cabbage
1 leek, white part only, diced

Who would believe that potatoes and cabbage combined with a few other well-chosen ingredients could seem so heavenly? This is Irish country food at its very simple best, from Executive Chef Tim Gurtner.

In an ovenproof medium saucepan over medium heat, place potatoes, cream, garlic, parsley, salt and pepper. Cook, stirring occasionally until mixture comes to a boil, about 5 minutes. Cover and bake in pre-heated 400° oven for 20 minutes.

While mixture bakes, blanch cabbage and leeks in boiling, salted water in a small saucepan just until tender, about 1 minute. Drain well, discarding liquid. Fold cabbage and leeks into potato mixture.

52 STAFFORD
52 Stafford Street
Plymouth, Wisconsin

Red Cabbage

makes 8 servings

2 tablespoons olive or
   safflower oil
1 large onion, sliced
1 large head red cabbage,
   shredded, about 7 cups
1 teaspoon whole cloves
4 bay leaves
1 pound McIntosh apples, peeled,
   cored and sliced ¼-inch thick
1½ cups beef broth
2 tablespoons apple cider
   vinegar
1-2 tablespoons sugar

Cafe Mozart is a small, out-of-the-way cafe that specializes in mostly German and Swiss food with a bit of French for good measure. Owner Eva-Maria Coughlin works with honest, quality ingredients in her family owned and operated restaurant. Her gracious hospitality permeates this cozy, charming cafe that promises "a taste to remember" in every carefully prepared dish.

In a 5-quart heavy kettle, heat the oil over medium/high heat until hot but not smoking, about 2½ minutes. Add onion and sauté for 5 minutes, stirring constantly. Stir in cabbage and apples. Tie cloves and 4 bay leaves in center of a 5-inch square of cheesecloth to make a bouquet garni. Toss into kettle and stir in broth.

Bring to a boil; reduce heat to simmer. Simmer for 45 minutes, stirring occasionally. Taste, adding vinegar and sugar to please your taste. Simmer for 10 more minutes. Remove bouquet garni. The flavors improve on the second day so this is a side dish that can be made in advance.

CAFE MOZART
311 West Main Street
Durand, Wisconsin

Sweet Potato, Artichoke and Parsnip Galette

makes 4 servings

2 cups heavy whipping cream
½ teaspoon dried leaf thyme
1 teaspoon salt or to taste
  (divided)
½ teaspoon white pepper
  (divided)
1½ pounds sweet potato, peeled
1 pound Idaho baking potatoes,
  peeled
12 ounces parsnips, peeled
6 large fresh artichoke hearts,
  cooked al dente
½ cup unsalted butter plus 4
  teaspoons (divided)
1 large yellow onion, cut in
  julienne
2 butternut squash, peeled,
  seeded, chopped
1 cup grated Asiago cheese

L'ETOILE
25 North Pinckney
Madison, Wisconsin

Creating a galette can be akin to culinary architecture. This multi-layered, beautifully crafted combination of fall vegetables comes to the table designed to get guests' attention. But it is the skillful blending of flavors that they will remember.

In a heavy 4-quart non-reactive saucepan, combine cream, thyme, ¼ teaspoon salt and ⅛ teaspoon pepper over medium heat and reduce mixture by one-fourth.

While cream mixture reduces, *separately* slice sweet potatoes, potatoes, parsnips and artichoke hearts very thin (¹⁄₁₆-inch) on mandoline and set aside. Place sliced potatoes in cold water; set aside.

Place parsnips and artichoke hearts in reduced cream mixture. Return mixture to a boil over medium/low heat. (It will cook the parsnips and artichokes and simultaneously reduce cream until it begins to "bind"—really thicken.) Check periodically and reduce heat if it begins to scorch. When fully reduced so cream clings to vegetables, spread vegetables on a baking sheet and cool.

Melt ½ cup butter in small pan. Set aside. Butter a 9- or 10-inch glass pie dish with 1 teaspoon butter.

Drain and pat potatoes dry. Place slices of sweet potato in center of pie dish and layer, working outward in a concentric circle. Brush with melted butter. Repeat layer using ⅓ of potatoes and melted butter. Sprinkle with salt and pepper.

Spread the cooled artichoke/parsnip/ cream mixture on these two layers. Press down. Make three layers each of sweet potatoes and potatoes, sprinkling with salt and pepper after first sweet potato layer and brushing with butter after completing each layer. Cover with aluminum foil and bake in preheated 400° oven about 55 minutes or until tender.

Make squash puree by slowly sautéing onions in large skillet with remaining 3 teaspoons butter, ⅛ teaspoon salt and ⅛ teaspoon white pepper until most of moisture has evaporated from onions. Do not brown onions. When onion just begins to brown, add squash. Reduce heat to low and simmer, covered, until squash is very tender, about 10 minutes. Cool; puree in food processor. Set aside.

Remove galette from oven; cool slightly and flip out onto a baking sheet. Top with cheese. Reheat at 400° for about 30 minutes. Slice in wedges and serve with steamed asparagus, sautéed spinach and reheated butternut squash puree.

Ratatouille - Grill Style

makes 5 cups

1 pound eggplant, trimmed,
  sliced lengthwise
1 pound zucchini, trimmed,
  sliced lengthwise
½ pound large yellow onion,
  trimmed, sliced ¼-inch thick
¼ pound red bell pepper, cut into
  large flat pieces
¼ pound green bell pepper, cut
  into large flat pieces
¼ cup olive oil (divided)
1 cup Chunky Tomato Relish (see
  recipe on page 129)
2 teaspoons crushed garlic
1½ teaspoons fresh minced basil
1 teaspoon salt
½ teaspoon freshly ground black
  pepper

You may have had this vegetable ragout from the south of France before, but grilling the vegetables adds a new dimension. The recipe from Christy and Craig uses a tomato relish from the Wilson Street Grill as one of its components. Make them both as you will love the flavors and find additional uses for the relish.

Sprinkle sliced eggplant and zucchini liberally with salt, let stand 30 minutes. Squeeze to remove excess moisture; blot off with paper towels. Set aside.

Preheat grill to high temperature. Brush eggplant, zucchini, onion and peppers with 2 tablespoons olive oil. Grill lightly on both sides, turning once, just enough to get grill marks and have some noticeable browning of vegetables, about 2-3 minutes per side.

Cut grilled eggplant, squash and peppers into 2-inch long by ⅜-inch wide pieces. Separate onion rings but leave whole. Place vegetables in large non-aluminum saucepan. Set aside.

Combine tomato relish, garlic, basil and remaining 2 tablespoons olive oil, adding salt and pepper to taste, if desired. Add to vegetable mixture; toss to coat. Cook over medium heat until tender but not soft, about 6 minutes. Serve hot.

WILSON STREET GRILL
217 South Hamilton
Madison, Wisconsin

Pasta Flans

makes 8 servings

10 ounces angel hair pasta,
   cooked, drained and cooled
3 large eggs
1 cup heavy whipping cream
¼ teaspoon salt
⅛ teaspoon dried leaf thyme,
   crumbled
½ teaspoon fresh minced garlic
⅛ teaspoon white pepper
½ cup grated Parmesan cheese

If you love pasta but wish there was a Miss Manners way to serve it to dinner guests, here's a lovely solution from Sous Chef Angela Hope. Cook the pasta in advance and combine quickly with the remaining ingredients to make these sweet little side dishes that come to the table in such a tidy fashion.

Prepare angel hair pasta according to package instructions; set aside.

In a medium bowl, mix together eggs and whipping cream with a wire whisk about 1 minute. Add salt, thyme, garlic, pepper and cheese. Whisk until thoroughly mixed, about 1 minute.

Spray 8 muffin tins with vegetable spray. Fill each muffin cup three-fourths full of pasta. Spoon egg mixture over top of pasta until the muffin cup is filled.

Bake in a preheated 350° oven for 20 minutes. Let cool in muffin cups for 5 minutes before removing from cup and serving.

RED CIRCLE INN
N44 W33013 Watertown Plank Road
Nashotah, Wisconsin

Tortellini
with Bacon and Peas

makes 4 servings

14 ounces refrigerated cheese or
  meat-filled tortellini
4 slices lean bacon, diced
½ cup unsalted butter
½ cup diced onion
½ teaspoon minced garlic
2 teaspoons minced fresh
  parsley
2 cups heavy whipping cream
1 teaspoon salt
¼ teaspoon freshly ground black
  pepper
2 cups cooked fresh or frozen
  peas, drained
2 tablespoons freshly grated
  Parmesan cheese

Choose refrigerated cheese or meat-filled tortellini as the base of this speedy supper main dish. Bright green peas, a bit of bacon and a sprinkling of freshly grated Parmesan cheese make flavorful components.

Cook tortellini in rapidly boiling water in large saucepan according to package directions. Drain and set aside.

In a 9-inch diameter skillet, sauté diced bacon over medium/high heat until crisp. Remove bacon bits to paper towel and drain.

Add butter to skillet and sauté onion, garlic and parsley until onion is translucent, about 1 minute. Stir in cream, salt and pepper and cook over medium heat to reduce to thickness of medium white sauce.

Add peas, reserved tortellini, reserved bacon and Parmesan cheese. Cook until heated through and cheese is incorporated.

THE RESTAURANT
1800 North Point Drive
Stevens Point, Wisconsin

Seasonal Beans
with Spinach and Bow Tie Pasta
makes 6 servings

Saffron Butter:

1 pound salted butter (divided)
1 pinch saffron
1 tablespoon minced garlic
1 tablespoon diced shallots
1 tablespoon red wine vinegar
½ cup white wine
1 tablespoon fresh lemon juice
1 bunch chopped parsley, stems
   removed, loosely packed,
   about 3 cups

Pasta:

1 pound fresh green beans,
   washed, ends trimmed
1 pound fresh yellow beans,
   washed, ends trimmed
1 pound fresh spinach leaves,
   washed, stems removed
1 cup white wine
2 teaspoons salt
2 teaspoons white pepper
1¼ cups Saffron Butter
6 ounces toasted sliced almonds
1 pound bow tie pasta, cooked to
   al dente stage

CAFE KNICKERBOCKER
1030 East Juneau Avenue
Milwaukee, Wisconsin

A seductive vegetarian entree created by Chef Rob Wagner that teams fresh beans, spinach and bow tie pasta in a buttery, rich sauce. You will have extra Saffron Butter left over. Store refrigerated, and use on any cooked vegetable you desire.

In a 9-inch diameter skillet or sauté pan, place saffron, garlic, shallots and 1 tablespoon of butter. Sauté over medium heat until shallots are translucent, about 2 minutes.

Add red wine vinegar, white wine and lemon juice and cook, reducing volume by three-fourths, about 10 minutes. Cool for 10 minutes. Place parsley, wine reduction and remaining nearly 1 pound of softened butter in food processor bowl fitted with metal blade or heavy mixer with beaters and incorporate butter at high speed, about 1 minute. Store in covered container. Set aside.

Heat sauté pan over medium/high heat and add beans and white wine. Cook, partially covered, stirring beans occasionally until beans are tender/crisp, about 4-5 minutes. Drain off white wine and discard.

Add spinach and 1¼ cups prepared Saffron Butter to pan and sauté until spinach is wilted and butter is melted, about 2 minutes. Gently mix in pasta to blend ingredients.

Divide mixture evenly between 6 warm plates and finish with a sprinkling of toasted almonds on top.

Red Beans and Rice

makes 8 servings

Cajun Seasoning:

2 teaspoons paprika
2 teaspoons salt
1 teaspoon cayenne
1 teaspoon black pepper
½ teaspoon leaf thyme, ground
1 teaspoon garlic powder
1 teaspoon onion powder

Beans and Rice:

1 ham bone
1 pound dried red beans
1 pound smoked sausage,
    preferably andouille
1 cup chopped onion
½ clove garlic, minced
2 teaspoons Cajun seasoning or
    to taste
8 cups water
8 cups cooked long grain white
    rice

This classic dish of New Orleans becomes something wonderful in Benny's Kitchen. The Chef includes his own Cajun seasoning recipe if you want to duplicate his flavors. And he is right about the importance of a ham bone.

Combine all Cajun seasoning ingredients together. Store in tightly sealed container.

Only a ham bone gives this dish its authentic color and flavor. In a large kettle, combine ham bone, red beans, smoked sausage, onion, garlic, Cajun seasoning and water. Bring to a boil over medium high heat; reduce heat to simmer. Cover and cook about 4 hours or until beans are tender. Serve over a bed of rice as main meal or side dish.

BENNY'S KITCHEN
239 West Main Street
Waukesha, Wisconsin

Wild Rice Stuffing

makes 6 servings

2 cups uncooked wild rice
4 cups chicken stock
6 tablespoons unsalted butter
   (divided)
1 cup diced onion
1 cup diced celery
Giblets from duckling, diced
1 teaspoon poultry seasoning
1 teaspoon fresh thyme or ½
   teaspoon dried leaf thyme
4 large eggs, beaten
8 ounces croutons (about 6 cups)
1 cup raisins, optional
1 teaspoon salt
½ teaspoon freshly ground black
   pepper

Serve this savory stuffing with Stout's Lodge recipe for Roast Duckling with Lingonberry Sauce on page 96. This is made as a side dish rather than the filling for the bird which is stuffed with fruit and spice for an infusion of flavors.

In a medium heavy saucepan, bring wild rice and chicken stock to a boil; reduce heat and simmer until grains of rice split open, about 35 minutes. (This should yield about 5 cups cooked wild rice.) Set aside.

In a 9-inch diameter skillet, heat 3 tablespoons butter and cook onion and celery, covered until tender. Stir in diced giblets, poultry seasoning and thyme.

In a 3-quart glass baking dish (dish should be no more than 3½ inches deep), combine rice mixture and vegetables. Stir in eggs and remaining 3 tablespoons of melted butter. Mix in croutons, raisins, salt, pepper and more stock if needed.

Bake, covered, in a preheated 350° oven for 30 minutes; uncover and bake for 15 minutes more. This is an excellent side dish with Stout's Lodge Roast Duckling.

STOUT'S LODGE
ISLAND OF HAPPY DAYS
Red Cedar Lake
Mikana, Wisconsin

Renaissance Rice

makes 6 servings

1 cup wild rice, rinsed and
  drained
1 teaspoon seasoning salt
1 cup brown rice*
7 cups water (divided)
2 teaspoons celery salt
1 teaspoon poultry seasoning
1 teaspoon white pepper
1 teaspoon onion powder
2 tablespoons butter or
  margarine
1 cup long grain white rice
Red or green onion, sliced
  thin—garnish
Toasted, slivered
  almonds—garnish

This tasty mixture of rices and seasoning is always served with The White Apron's Grilled Chicken Breast in Teriyaki Sauce. Garnish with red or green onions and slivered, toasted almonds as Chef Barbara McCarrier does.

In medium saucepan, bring 2½ cups of wild rice, water and seasoning salt to a boil. Reduce heat; cover and simmer for 40 minutes or until rice is tender-crisp, not mushy.

Meanwhile, combine brown rice, remaining 4½ cups water, celery salt, poultry seasoning, white pepper, onion powder and butter in large saucepan. Bring to a boil and simmer, covered, about 25 minutes. Stir in white rice and cook until rice is tender, about 20 minutes more.

Drain off any liquid remaining from rice mixtures; discard liquid. Combine wild rice mixture with mixed rice mixture. Garnish with sliced green or red onions and toasted almonds. Serve 1 cup rice with Grilled Chicken Breast Teriyaki and Vegetables, page 86.

* *If you use quick-cooking brown or white rices, adjust cooking time according to package instructions.*

THE WHITE APRON
414 Maple Drive
Sister Bay, Wisconsin

Eggs Florentine
with Mornay Sauce

makes 2 servings

Sauce:

2½ tablespoons unsalted butter
3 tablespoons flour
1 cup milk
½ cup whipping cream
½ teaspoon salt
⅛ teaspoon ground white pepper
⅛ teaspoon nutmeg
2 dashes hot pepper sauce
¼ cup grated Swiss cheese
¼ cup plus 2 tablespoons freshly
   grated Parmesan cheese
   (divided)

Eggs Florentine:

4 large eggs
1 pound fresh spinach, washed,
   stems removed, drained
1-2 tablespoons unsalted butter
½ teaspoon minced garlic
½ teaspoon salt
4 slices toast
4 tablespoons whipped butter
Orange wedges, whole
   strawberries, or other fresh
   fruit—garnish

**THE CHESTERFIELD INN
BED & BREAKSAST**
*20 Commerce Street
Mineral Point, Wisconsin*

This is a wonderful brunch dish that features fresh tender spinach, a marvelously seasoned Mornay Sauce and eggs poached to perfection. Garnish the plate with pretty fruits in season as the Inn and other Ovens of Brittany restaurants do.

To make sauce, melt butter in heavy saucepan; stir in flour until well-blended. Cook over low heat, stirring often for 3-5 minutes. Meanwhile, gently heat remaining sauce ingredients, except cheeses, in microwave or another small pan. Whisk milk mixture into flour mixture until smooth. Simmer about 10 minutes, stirring often. Remove from heat and stir in Swiss cheese and ¼ cup Parmesan cheese. Set aside.

In a 10-inch diameter buttered skillet, add enough hot water to a depth of 1½ inches. Bring to boil; reduce to simmer. Break eggs, one at a time in a saucer and slip into water. Cook for 3 to 5 minutes. Remove eggs with slotted spoon; drain. Keeping warm, set aside.

Clean skillet, melt 1-2 tablespoons butter in skillet and add garlic and spinach, stirring over medium heat until spinach wilts and is tender. Drain off moisture—keep warm.

Assemble Eggs Florentine by placing 2 slices of toast spread with whipped butter on each of 2 serving plates. Place one-half of spinach on each plate over toast. Top each serving with two poached eggs. Ladle 1 cup Mornay Sauce over each portion; sprinkle each plate with remaining Parmesan cheese. Garnish plates with fresh fruit.

Mexican Omelet

makes 4 omelets

Filling:

2 cans chopped green chilies (4
   ounces *each*), drained
2 tablespoons mayonnaise
4 tablespoons dairy sour cream
2-4 teaspoons hot salsa
4 tablespoons minced green
   onion
4 tablespoons minced green bell
   pepper
1 cup shredded Monterey Jack
   cheese
½ cup chopped black
   olives—garnish

Eggs:

8 tablespoons whipped unsalted
   butter or margarine (divided)
8 large eggs
½ cup cold water

THE KITCHEN TABLE
*East 3rd and Maple
Marshfield, Wisconsin*

An omelet with southwest roots. Follow the step-by-step instructions for making a perfect omelet. Serve salsa on the side to make an already delicious dish a real treat.

Make enough filling for 4 omelets by combining all ingredients in a small bowl; stir to blend. Set aside.

Heat 2 tablespoons butter in a 9 or 10-inch diameter skillet or omelet pan over medium heat until hot.

Whip eggs in small bowl with a fork, add water and whip for 5 seconds more.

Pour one-fourth of egg mixture into skillet, increase heat to high. Eggs should sizzle softly. Eggs will begin to cook on bottom in 5-10 seconds. Shake pan briskly and with a spatula push cooked egg to the center while tipping the pan and letting uncooked egg flow to the outside edges. Continue this motion until eggs no longer flow. (Center will be quite soft—this is okay.)

Remove from heat and add one-fourth of filling onto half of the omelet surface, adding cheese last. Put under a broiler in skillet until cheese melts and eggs are cooked and puffy, about 2 minutes. Turn out onto a warm plate, sliding filled half of omelet onto plate first. Flip the remaining omelet half from pan over top of filled omelet half. Garnish with black olives.

Repeat cooking procedure to make remaining 3 omelets.

POULTRY

Chicken Walnut Salad	80
Chicken Cashew Salad *with Balsamic Vinaigrette*	81
Grilled Chicken Salad *with Strawberry Vinaigrette*	82
Grilled Chicken and Vegetable Salad *with Herb Dressing*	84
Grilled Chicken Breast Teriyaki	86
Grilled Chicken Breast *with Lemon Sauce and Angel Hair Pasta*	87
Cilantro Chicken *with Papaya Salsa*	88
Nopalitos Con Queso	90
Kettle Moraine Stuffed Chicken Breast	92
Duck Breast Salad *with Raspberry Vinaigrette*	94
Oriental Duck and Pasta Salad	95
Roast Duckling *with Lingonberry Sauce*	96

Chicken Walnut Salad

makes 6 servings

Salad:

2 pounds cooked chicken, diced
½ cup celery, diced
½ cup onion, diced
1 can mandarin oranges (8 ounces), drained, reserve ¼ cup liquid
¾ cup toasted coconut
1 cup chopped walnuts

Dressing:

2½ cups mayonnaise
¼ cup reserved mandarin orange liquid
¼ cup orange juice
½ teaspoon salt or to taste
Freshly ground black pepper to taste

The Weissgerber family continues to satisfy diner's taste for German dishes like their classic Sauerbraten, Spätzle and Red Cabbage, but Chef Phil Haseker balances the menu nicely with entrees like this Chicken Walnut Salad.

In a large mixing bowl, combine chicken celery, onion, orange slices, coconut, walnuts. Set aside.

Make dressing by combining in medium bowl, mayonnaise, mandarin orange liquid, orange juice, salt and pepper.

Add salad dressing to salad mix; stir gently to combine. Chill, covered for 2 hours to blend flavors.

GASTHAUS RESTAURANT
2720 North Grandview Boulevard
Waukesha, Wisconsin

Chicken Cashew Salad
with Balsamic Vinaigrette
makes 4 servings

Vinaigrette:

1 cup balsamic vinegar
¼ cup Dijon-style mustard
1 tablespoon sugar
2¼ teaspoons salt
1 tablespoon crushed garlic
2¼ teaspoons freshly ground
    black pepper
¼ cup fresh lemon juice, strained
2 cups olive oil

Salad:

4 whole chicken breasts (6-
    ounces *each*), boned and
    skinned
1 whole red or green bell pepper
1 pound fresh spinach, washed,
    stemmed, drained
4 large fresh tomatoes, each cut
    in 6 wedges
4 hard cooked eggs, peeled and
    cut in 6 wedges
24 pitted black olives
4 ounces roasted cashews

THE OVENS OF BRITTANY
1718 Fordem Avenue
Madison, Wisconsin

Bright and beautiful, this refreshing main dish salad sports a sturdy dressing of balsamic vinegar, mustard and fresh lemon juice. Clean flavors, sterling fresh ingredients and roasted cashews guarantee raves for the cook.

Make vinaigrette in a medium mixing bowl, whisking together vinegar, mustard, sugar, salt, garlic, pepper and lemon juice. Slowly whisk in olive oil in a thin stream, whisking until all oil is incorporated into an emulsion. Store, covered, in an airtight container. Makes about 3½ cups vinaigrette.

Marinate chicken breasts and whole pepper in 2 cups of vinaigrette in large plastic self-sealing bag for at least 1 hour. Reserve remaining dressing for use on salad. Drain chicken and pepper, discarding dressing. Grill on hot grill about 6 minutes per side for chicken, turning once. Turn pepper until grill marks are visible on all sides.

Remove chicken and pepper to clean cutting board. Place pepper in plastic self-sealing bag to soften skin. When chicken is somewhat cooled, slice each breast into 6-7 slices. Remove skin from pepper; discard skin. Cut pepper into ¼-inch wide lengthwise strips; discarding stem, seeds and white membrane. Set aside.

Divide spinach evenly between 4 salad plates. Alternate wedges of tomato and egg around center of plate. Add olives between wedges. Top salad with marinated slices of chicken and pepper strips. Top with cashews. Drizzle with reserved dressing.

Grilled Chicken Salad
with Strawberry Vinaigrette

makes 4 servings

Vinaigrette:

12 cups fresh or unsweetened
   frozen strawberries, pureed
6-8 tablespoons sugar
1½ teaspoons paprika
1½ teaspoons salt
¾ teaspoon dry mustard
Dash of white pepper
1 cup red wine vinegar
¼ cup fresh lemon juice, strained
2 tablespoons diced onion
4 teaspoons Worcestershire
   sauce
1 cup vegetable oil
1 cup olive oil

Chicken Salad:

4 whole chicken breasts (6-8
   ounces *each*) skinned, boned
8 cups mixed salad greens, torn
   in bite-size pieces, washed and
   drained

THE INN AT CEDAR CROSSING
336 Louisiana Street
Sturgeon Bay, Wisconsin

This is a gorgeous salad that combines fresh summer flavors in a simple, yet smashing presentation. Use fresh strawberries to make the vinaigrette that separately marinates the chicken and flavors the salad. Pound the chicken breasts to uniform thickness as the directions suggest and do not overcook. Make this when berries are in season.

In a large mixing bowl with electric mixer, combine pureed strawberries, sugar, paprika, salt, dry mustard, white pepper, vinegar, lemon juice, onion and Worcestershire sauce until well-blended.

Slowly whisk in (or using low speed on electric mixer) vegetable and olive oils in a thin stream until incorporated and mixture forms an emulsion. Blend for 5 minutes. Set aside.

Place chicken breasts on plastic or glass cutting surface; cover with plastic wrap. Lightly pound until chicken breasts are uniform thickness of about ½-inch. Place chicken in heavy self-sealing plastic bag or in shallow glass dish; pour one-half of strawberry vinaigrette over to cover. Seal or cover and let marinate in refrigerator for at least 4 hours.

Drain chicken breasts, discarding marinade. Preheat grill to high temperature. Brush grill lightly with vegetable oil. Grill chicken over hot coals turning once, 4-5 minutes per side. Remove from grill, cool slightly and cut into bite-size pieces.

Divide chilled greens between 4 salad plates. Top each plate of greens with one-fourth of chicken pieces. Drizzle with strawberry vinaigrette. Garnish, if desired, with whole fresh strawberries.

Grilled Chicken and Vegetable Salad
with Herb Dressing

makes 4 servings

Dressing:

1½ cups red wine vinegar
½ cup balsamic vinegar
4 cloves garlic, crushed
1 tablespoon freshly ground
 black pepper
1 tablespoon minced fresh
 rosemary
2 tablespoons minced fresh basil
1 tablespoon sugar
2 cups extra-virgin olive oil

Salad:

1 pound boned and skinned
 chicken breasts
2 small zucchini, washed and
 drained
2 small yellow squash, washed
 and drained
8 large mushrooms, cleaned and
 trimmed
2 small red onions
1 red bell pepper
1 green bell pepper
6 cups torn romaine lettuce,
 washed, drained and chilled

QUIVEY'S GROVE
6261 Nesbitt Road
Madison, Wisconsin

Everyone wants to find more ways to cook chicken breasts that are light and yet flavorful. Try this herb-based vinaigrette that is used partially as marinade and partially as dressing for this colorful melange of grilled chicken and vegetables. A good choice when your guests include vegetarians as the chicken can be optional—a special salad from Master Chef Craig Kuenning.

In a blender or mixing bowl with whisk, combine all salad dressing ingredients until blended. Measure out ½ cup of dressing to use as marinade; set remaining dressing in refrigerator to chill.

Place chicken breasts in shallow glass container and pour ½ cup dressing over chicken. Cover with plastic wrap; place in refrigerator for at least 2 hours.

Cut zucchini and yellow squash in lengthwise halves; then cut crosswise in half to make 8 pieces of each. Peel red onions, leaving the root ends on. Cut each into quarters. Clean and seed pepper, cutting each into 8 lengthwise strips.

Place all vegetables in a glass or stainless steel bowl; add 1 cup reserved dressing and let marinate in refrigerator for 1 hour.

In a small saucepan, heat remaining 1½ cups dressing over low heat until warm. Keep warm. Drain marinade from chicken breasts and grill over hot coals, turning once, until done, about 6 minutes per side. Drain and grill all vegetables over hot coals turning once, until tender, about 4-5 minutes per side.

Divide lettuce between 4 plates, mounding in center. Slice squash into bite-size pieces and place in center of lettuce. Arrange remainder of vegetables around lettuce. Slice chicken breasts in ½-inch thick slices and arrange over salad. Ladle warm dressing over each and serve immediately.

Grilled Chicken Breast Teriyaki

makes 4 servings

Teriyaki Sauce:

1 cup soy sauce
1 cup vegetable oil
½ cup brown sugar
⅔ cup cherry juice or dry
 sherry
1 tablespoon fresh ginger,
 grated
2 teaspoons fresh garlic,
 minced
1 teaspoon Chinese Five
 Spices
1 tablespoon roasted dark
 sesame oil (Oriental)

Chicken Breast:

4 whole chicken breasts,
 boned, skinned (6 ounces
 each)

Vegetables:

1½ cups fresh broccoli florets,
 washed and drained
1½ cups fresh cauliflower
 florets, washed and drained
1 cup peeled carrots, sliced
 ¼-inch

One of the most popular items on the menu is Chef Barbara McCarrier's Grilled Chicken Breast Teriyaki which she serves with fresh vegetables subtly seasoned with Teriyaki Sauce and Renaissance Rice as a side dish.

Combine Teriyaki Sauce ingredients together in medium bowl with wire whisk. Place chicken breasts in self-sealing plastic bag; add 2 cups sauce and marinate for 1 hour. Remove from marinade; drain and grill over hot coals or gas grill on medium-high temperature for 5 minutes per side or until juices run clear.

In a 9-inch diameter skillet sauté raw vegetables in ½ cup Teriyaki Sauce until tender-crisp, about 5 minutes. Serve 1 cup vegetables with each grilled chicken breast and Renaissance Rice, page 76, if you wish.

THE WHITE APRON
414 Maple Drive
Sister Bay, Wisconsin

Grilled Chicken Breast
with Lemon Sauce and Angel Hair Pasta

makes 4 servings

Sauce:

4 tablespoons butter
4 tablespoons flour
3 cups chicken stock
½ cup Chablis wine
1 lemon, washed

Chicken Breast:

4 chicken breast halves (4
    ounces *each*), skinned,
    boned and pounded ¼-inch
    thick

Pasta:

8 ounces angel hair pasta,
    cooked and drained
4 tablespoons minced shallots,
    about 2 large shallots
2 tablespoons butter

I enjoyed Chef Tom D'Olivo's light and lovely entree on my birthday this May on Maria's sunny outdoor patio. The flavors are perfect in this pretty dish— and it is simple to assemble and serve.

Make sauce by melting butter in medium saucepan. Whisk in flour until blended. Let cook for 2 minutes, stirring constantly. Gradually whisk in chicken stock and wine. Grate zest from lemon; set aside. Squeeze juice from lemon (you will need about 4 tablespoons juice) and whisk into sauce. Cook over medium/high heat, stirring constantly until thickened, about 3 minutes. Whisk in zest at end of cooking; set aside.

Grill chicken breasts over hot coals or on high setting of gas grill, about 3 minutes per side or until juices run clear. Remove to warm serving plate.

Sauté shallots and 2 tablespoons butter together in small skillet until shallots are transparent, about 2 minutes. Mix into cooked pasta. Divide pasta and chicken breasts among four serving plates. Pour ¼ of sauce over each chicken breast and drizzle over pasta.

MARIA'S ITALIAN CUISINE
159 West Wisconsin Avenue
Oconomowoc, Wisconsin

Cilantro Chicken
with Papaya Salsa
makes 6-8 servings

Cilantro Chicken:

2 chickens, quartered or 8 whole skinned and boned chicken breasts (6-8 ounces *each*)
1 cup fresh lime juice
1 cup fresh lemon juice
1½ cups dry white wine
½ cup olive oil
1½ cups chopped cilantro
4 cloves garlic, minced
1 tablespoon fresh chopped rosemary
1 tablespoon fresh chopped tarragon
1 tablespoon coarsely ground black pepper
2 teaspoons coarse sea salt
3 ripe avocados, peeled and pitted, sliced ¼-inch thick—garnish
2 vine-ripened tomatoes, sliced ¼-inch thick—garnish
Fresh cilantro leaves—garnish

Salsa:

2 ripe papayas (about 1 pound *each*)
1 jalapeno pepper, red or green
1 large clove garlic, peeled and minced
½ cup finely chopped red onion
¼ cup chopped cilantro
½ cup fresh lime juice, strained
1 cup peeled, chopped pineapple

This marinated chicken is oven baked to golden brown tenderness and served with a brightly colored fresh salsa. If you are looking for a light, yet flavorful new dish with chicken, this is it. You can use a whole fryer or chicken breasts, as you wish.

Place chicken pieces in a large, shallow non-aluminum pan. Combine lime and lemon juices, wine, olive oil, cilantro, garlic, rosemary, tarragon, pepper and sea salt and pour over chicken. Cover; refrigerate for 2 hours, stirring several times to season.

Make papaya salsa by peeling papayas and discarding seeds and peel. Cube papaya ½-inch in size and place in medium bowl. Wear kitchen gloves while handling pepper. Remove and discard seeds and membrane. Dice pepper. Add to papaya along with garlic, onion, cilantro, lime juice and pineapple. Cover tightly and chill at least 4 hours before serving.

THE OLD RITTENHOUSE INN
301 Rittenhouse Avenue
Bayfield, Wisconsin

Remove chicken from marinade, reserving 2 tablespoons of marinade to place with chicken in 13″ x 9″ x 2″ baking dish. Bake, covered, in preheated 350° oven for 15 minutes. Remove cover and bake until fork tender, about 25 minutes more or until juices run clear when chicken is pierced with a fork.

Transfer chicken to warm serving platter. Garnish with overlapping slices of avocado and tomato. Serve with Papaya Salsa.

Nopalitos Con Queso

makes 4 servings

4 whole chicken breasts
   (6 ounces *each*) skinned and
   boned
¼ cup vegetable oil
16 large raw shrimp, peeled and
   deveined
1 large onion, sliced
32 ounces diced cactus, rinsed
   thoroughly (refer to text)
2 cups chile ancho pulp (refer to
   text)
½ cup tomato sauce
¼ cup water
2 tablespoons minced fresh
   garlic
1 teaspoon salt
2 teaspoons chili powder
½ teaspoon cumin
2 cups mild Cheddar cheese

Owner Ada Lara de Thimke wanted cooks to know that cooking with cactus is common and very popular throughout all of Mexico, so she enclosed some information for novice cooks. According to Ada, cactus is used in a variety of ways from soups, salads and entrees to jellies, juices and even candy.

At Lara's Tortilla Flats, a salad and two entrees are made with cactus. The most popular one is this recipe (Cactus with Cheese).

All of the ingredients required for this dish can be found in any Hispanic market or the larger supermarkets that carry Mexican goods.

Two ingredients in this dish need further explanation before the dish can be prepared.

Nopalitos (cactus) can be bought two ways, canned or fresh.

Canned cactus is already cleaned, cooked, diced and spiced. The oil and liquid with the cactus will seem sticky. Lara assures us this is perfectly natural. Place cactus in a strainer and run cold water over it until it is thoroughly rinsed.

If you are an adventurous cook and would like to try fresh cactus, Ada offers the following information. You will find cactus in the produce department. Pick firm, fresh (not droopy or wrinkled) leaves. Rinse pads well; pat dry. Brush each side with oil. Salt lightly. Cook on a griddle for 20-25 minutes over medium/low heat, turning occasionally, or roast in a 350° oven for 25-30 minutes. Cool and cut into strips.

Chile Ancho Pulp is made from dried chile ancho pods. (Wear kitchen gloves whenever handling hot peppers and wash your hands with cool water when done.) Rinse pods under running water to remove any dust. Soak in warm water until pliable (1-2 hours). Remove seeds and puree in a blender with enough water just to cover pods. Strain. Pulp has a bitter taste at this point but is wonderful when used in sauces, like the following recipe.

LARA'S TORTILLA FLATS
715 North Main Street
Oshkosh, Wisconsin

On plastic or glass cutting surface, cut chicken into strips about 2-inches long and ½-inch wide. In a 10-inch diameter deep skillet or large sauté pan, heat oil and sauté chicken over medium/high heat, turning strips and cooking for about 2 minutes per side until almost done. Add shrimp; sauté until opaque, about 3 minutes.

Add cactus and onion to chicken mixture. Cook over medium heat, stirring constantly. Add ancho pulp, tomato sauce and water; stir well and simmer for 2 minutes. Add garlic, salt, chili powder and cumin; stir to blend flavors. Add cheese; simmer over low heat for about 3 minutes. Serve with rice, beans and hot tortillas.

Kettle Moraine
Stuffed Chicken Breast

makes 6 servings

Sauce:

1 cup half-and-half
1 tablespoon cornstarch
1 tablespoon water
½ cup tangy prepared
   barbecue sauce (divided)
6 ounces brick cheese (divided)
¼ teaspoon salt
¼ teaspoon freshly ground
   black pepper

Chicken with Stuffing:

6 whole chicken breasts
   (6 ounces *each*), boned,
   skinned, and trimmed of any
   visible fat
6 ounces smoked pork loin
¾ cup corn meal
¾ cup flour
1 teaspoon garlic powder
½ teaspoon white pepper
1 teaspoon salt
3 large eggs
½ cup canola or corn oil

HEAVEN CITY RESTAURANT
S91 W27850 National Avenue
Mukwonago, Wisconsin

This recipe, notes Chef Scott Mc-Glinchey, is a favorite at Heaven City Restaurant. They smoke locally raised Maple Creek Farm pork loin over apple and maple woods and stuff chicken breasts with the pork, their tangy homemade barbecue sauce and Wisconsin brick cheese. It is rolled in corn meal and gently sautéed until golden and served on a tangy barbecue, cheese cream sauce. It has become the restaurant's biggest seller.

Make barbecue sauce by heating half-and-half in small saucepan over medium/high heat. Bring to a boil and add cornstarch that has been mixed with water. Reduce heat; simmer for 2 minutes. Add ¼ cup barbecue sauce and 3 ounces cheese, mixing until smooth. Season with salt and pepper. Set aside.

Pound out chicken breasts to a heart shape, about ¼-inch thick. Set aside. Slice pork loin thin and cut into julienne (matchstick cuts) and toss with remaining ¼ cup barbecue sauce.

Place chicken breasts, skinned side down on cookie sheet, layering 1 ounce of smoked pork loin and ½ ounce of brick cheese on one side of chicken breast. Fold the other side of breast over creating a pocket. Press around edges to seal.

Cover with foil and freeze on pan for one hour. Place ½ cup of flour on paper plate; set aside. Beat eggs in medium bowl; set aside. Place corn meal, remaining ¼ cup flour, garlic powder, salt and white pepper on another paper plate and whisk together.

Roll the frozen stuffed chicken breasts in flour, then dip into eggs, then cornmeal mixture. Pour oil in large skillet and heat over medium/high heat. Sauté chicken breasts until golden on both sides, about 15-20 minutes.

Place browned chicken breasts on cookie sheet and bake in preheated 425° oven for 5-10 minutes or until juices run clear when meat is pierced with a fork or chicken feels firm when touched. To serve, place a pool of barbecue sauce on each plate, place chicken breast centered on pool. Serve hot.

Duck Breast Salad
with Raspberry Vinaigrette
makes 4 servings

Vinaigrette:

¼ cup raspberry vinegar
1 small shallot, chopped fine
1 small clove garlic, mashed
½ teaspoon salt
½ teaspoon freshly ground black
    pepper
1 teaspoon sugar
2 teaspoons sauterne wine
¾ cup walnut oil

Duck Salad:

12 ounces duck breasts, boned,
    skinned (reserve skin)
4 ounces walnut halves, about
    1 cup
1 tablespoon butter
2 stalks celery, cut in fine
    julienne
2 ounces green onion, cut in fine
    julienne, about ½ cup
½ cup dried cherries
1 small red apple, diced
4 cups Napa cabbage, cut in
    chiffonade
6 cups torn salad greens,
    washed, drained and chilled
½ pint fresh raspberries

QUIVEY'S GROVE
6261 Nesbitt Road
Madison, Wisconsin

So pretty we put it on the cover of our cookbook, and so tasty that our testers cleaned their plates and asked for this recipe from Master Chef Craig Kuenning. Brilliant colors, crisp textures and properly upscale ingredients make this a main dish salad to remember for special occasions.

To make vinaigrette, combine all ingredients (except oil) in blender or bowl with whisk. Whisk in oil in slow, steady stream until vinaigrette thickens and all oil is incorporated. Set aside.

In a 9-inch diameter skillet or sauté pan, fry the reserved duck skin to get 1 tablespoon duck fat; discard skin. Sauté the duck breasts in hot duck fat over medium heat 4-5 minutes then turn and sauté for 3 minutes more until medium rare. Cool on plate; slice in ¼-inch thick cuts or julienne. Set aside.

In a heavy medium saucepan, sauté walnuts in butter until well roasted and aromatic, 2 minutes. Drain on paper towels; cool. Toss the walnuts, celery, green onion, cherries and apples together. Whisk dressing and pour over walnut mixture.

Divide the cabbage and salad greens between four chilled salad plates. Place ¼ of walnut mixture on top of greens on each plate. Fan out duck breast slices in center of plate. Garnish with raspberries.

Oriental Duck and Pasta Salad

makes 4 servings

Marinade:

1 cup rice vinegar
½ cup Rhine wine
½ cup soy sauce
½ cup sugar
½ cup sliced onion
1 tablespoon grated fresh ginger
   or 1 teaspoon ground ginger
2 cloves garlic, minced, about 2
   teaspoons
½ teaspoon paprika

Duck Salad:

¼ cup dark or roasted sesame oil
2 cups boneless cooked duck
   breast meat, slivered
2 large carrots, cut in julienne
   strips
½ pound snow pea pods, trimmed
½ pound zucchini, cut in julienne
   strips
1 pound linguine
Romaine and leaf lettuce,
   washed and chilled
5-6 slivered scallions
1 cup diced red pepper
2 tablespoons toasted sesame
   seeds

A rainbow of color with Far Eastern flavors sets this duck breast salad apart from others you've tasted. Don't hesitate to buy duck breasts, either frozen or fresh in quality meat markets. They are solid, chubby little bundles that sauté quickly (about 8 minutes total for a pink center) and add so much flavor to any dish.

In a small saucepan, combine ingredients for marinade and cook over medium heat for 5 minutes. Cool slightly. Marinate duck meat in 1¼ cups of sauce.

Add sesame oil to remaining sauce; reserve. Prepare carrots, pea pods, and zucchini. Set aside. Cook linguine according to package directions and drain. Toss with reserve sauce/oil mixture.

Drain marinade from duck, discarding marinade and add meat to pasta along with vegetables. Arrange one-fourth of lettuce on each of four chilled salad plates. Divide pasta mixture evenly among plates. Garnish each plate with scallions, red pepper and toasted sesame seeds.

**KARL RATZSCH'S
OLD WORLD RESTAURANT**
*320 East Mason Street
Milwaukee, Wisconsin*

Roast Duckling
with Lingonberry Sauce
makes 2 generous servings

1 duckling (3-4 pounds)
1 teaspoon salt
½ teaspoon cracked black pepper
1 lemon, cut in quarters
½ orange, cut in half
1 tablespoon cracked fennel seed
Juice of 1 lemon
Lingonberry Sauce*

Roast duckling emerges with the clean citrus and fennel flavors of its unusual stuffing. It is a tasty departure from the ordinary and one our test staff particularly enjoyed.

Rinse duckling under cold water, remove and discard any loose fat. Reserve giblets to make Wild Rice Stuffing on page 75. Pat carcass dry with paper towels. Rub inside cavity with salt and cracked pepper.

Stuff cavity with lemon quarters, orange pieces and fennel seed. Rub outer skin with lemon juice. Place on a roasting rack in a roasting pan, breast up. Roast in a preheated 450° oven for 15 minutes. Reduce heat to 350°. Roast for 1 hour or until the leg feels loose and pliable when twisted.

Let duck cool on plastic or glass cutting surface. Cut in half; serve each half with warmed Lingonberry Sauce and Wild Rice Stuffing.

* *Lingonberry Sauce is available in specialty food stores.*

**STOUT'S LODGE
ISLAND OF HAPPY DAYS**
*Red Cedar Lake
Mikana, Wisconsin*

FISH AND SEAFOOD

Grilled Smoked Salmon
with Fresh Dill Caper Mustard

makes 4 servings

Grilled Salmon:

4 salmon steaks or fillets (4
 ounces *each*)
½ teaspoon salt or to taste
¼ teaspoon freshly ground black
 pepper
5 or 6 large hardwood chips,
 soaked in water for 10
 minutes

Mustard:

½ cup Dijon-style mustard
½ cup olive oil
1 tablespoon capers
2 tablespoons fresh dill, minced
 or 1 tablespoon dried dill
 weed
3 small cloves minced garlic
⅛ teaspoon freshly ground black
 pepper
Fresh lemon slices—garnish
Fresh sprigs of dill—garnish

Do try flavoring this grilled salmon with pre-soaked hardwood chips. Somehow, the wood smoke adds heartiness to an otherwise delicate salmon. Chef/owner Jim Jensen suggests that this dish could be used as an entree as well as an appetizer.

Prepare grill to a medium temperature. Place pre-soaked wood chips on top of hot coals in the center of grill. Sprinkle surface of fillets lightly with salt and pepper, if desired and spray surfaces with vegetable oil spray.

Place salmon on grill around edge of wood chips. Cover, close vents to avoid flame-ups, and grill without turning until cooked, about 8-9 minutes. Flesh should be opaque throughout.

While salmon cooks, make sauce by whisking mustard in small bowl. Slowly whisk in oil in a thin stream until oil is all absorbed in the emulsion. Mix in capers, dill weed, garlic, salt and pepper. Arrange salmon on plate, serve with a dollop (2 tablespoons) of dill caper mustard and garnish with lemon slices or fresh sprigs of dill, if desired.

THE VINTAGE
3110 8th Street South
Wisconsin Rapids, Wisconsin

Poached Salmon
with Shiitake Mushroom Sauce

makes 4 servings

4 tablespoons Herb Butter*
4 fresh salmon fillets, deboned
   (6 ounces *each*)
2 cups Court Bouillon*
16 large shiitake mushrooms,
   cleaned and stems removed
4 tablespoons unsalted butter
2 tablespoons chopped shallots
½ cup cream sherry
1 cup Veal Demi-Glace*

I hope you'll take the time to put all the components together for this stunning salmon entree. I confess the process is daunting and I wondered if I would be satisfied with the end results. In retrospect, I never should have questioned Chef Paul J. Short III's endeavor. The results are magnificent.

Divide Herb Butter into 4 equal pieces and place 4 inches apart on bottom of a 13″ x 9″ x 2″ glass baking dish. Place a salmon fillet on top of each piece of Herb Butter. Gently pour Court Bouillon over salmon and place in a preheated 400° oven.

Bake for about 12-15 minutes or until beads of white form on surface of salmon. Salmon should be opaque throughout. Place salmon fillets on warm serving platter and drain off most of the bouillon, reserving about ¼ cup. Cover salmon to retain warmth.

In a medium saucepan, place mushrooms, butter and shallots with reserved ¼ cup Court Bouillon. Bring to boil over high heat and add sherry and reduce liquid by one-half. Add Demi-Glace, cook for 5 seconds more. Spoon a few mushrooms over each fillet and pour sauce over fillets. Serve immediately.

THE SANDHILL INN
170 East Main Street, Hwy. 78
Merrimac, Wisconsin

* *Sandhill Inn recipes for these are found in this cookbook. Refer to pages 131, 132 and 134.*

Marinated Grilled Smoked Tuna
with Roasted Red Pepper Melange

makes 4 servings

Red Pepper Melange:

3-4 medium red bell peppers
½ cup white wine
¼ teaspoon salt (divided)
¼ teaspoon fresh ground black
   pepper (divided)

Marinade:

4 tablespoons vinegar
4 tablespoons olive oil
1 teaspoon diced onion
½ teaspoon minced garlic
2 tablespoons liquid smoke
2 tablespoons fresh lemon juice

Steaks:

4 tuna steaks (6-8 ounces *each*),
   1-inch thick

Stretch your grilling repertoire with fresh tuna and roasted sweet red bell peppers. You'll love the smoke-infused flavors from this attractive pairing. Remember not to overcook the tuna. It is best when still slightly pink in the center.

Roast whole peppers on hot grill or in broiler, turning until skin blisters and darkens on all sides. Remove peppers, place immediately in a self-sealing plastic bag and let stand for 15 minutes.

Remove all charred skin from peppers. (Rinsing under cold water may aid this process.) Cut into quarters and remove and discard seeds and white membranes. Cut peppers into julienne strips and place in small saucepan with wine. Heat over low heat. Taste and season with ⅛ teaspoon salt and ⅛ teaspoon pepper, if desired. Set aside.

In a small bowl, combine vinegar, olive oil, onion, garlic, remaining ⅛ teaspoon salt, remaining ⅛ teaspoon black pepper, liquid smoke and lemon juice. Whisk together until well-blended. Place tuna steaks in shallow glass dish or in self-sealing plastic bag. Pour marinade over all, turning to coat. Refrigerate for 1½ to 2 hours.

RED GERANIUM RESTAURANT
7194 Highway 50 R
Lake Geneva, Wisconsin

Drain marinade from steaks, reserving marinade to brush on steaks halfway through grilling process. Grill over gas or charcoal on high heat about 4 minutes per side. Brush with reserved marinade after turning steaks. Grill medium rare (center should be light pink) for best texture and flavor.

Transfer tuna to warm plates or serving platter and top with reserved red pepper melange.

Sautéed Grouper Cheeks
on Rice Tabbouleh with Tomato Vinaigrette
makes 4 servings

Rice Tabbouleh:
3½ tablespoons olive oil
2 tablespoons finely diced
  onions
¼ bay leaf
¼ cup rice, uncooked
⅓ cup chicken stock (salted to
  taste)
2 plum tomatoes, about 4 ounces
  total
1 scallion, finely diced
¼ teaspoon ground coriander
1 cup parsley tops, chopped
  coarsely, loosely packed
1 tablespoon lemon juice
2 tablespoons extra virgin olive
  oil
Salt to taste
Freshly ground black pepper to
  taste

Vinaigrette:
½ cup olive oil
3 tablespoons rice wine vinegar
4 plum tomatoes, peeled, seeded
  and diced small, about 8
  ounces
⅓ teaspoon salt
⅛ teaspoon freshly ground black
  pepper
2 tablespoons mixed chopped
  chives and chiffonade of mint

Grouper Cheeks:
24 ounces grouper cheeks
½ cup flour
½ teaspoon salt
¼ teaspoon freshly ground black
  pepper
⅓ cup olive oil

Make this beautiful Tabbouleh ahead as well as the Tomato Vinaigrette. Last minute cooking only involves the quick sautéing of delicate pure white grouper cheeks. Request them in advance from your local fish market, suggests Chef Sanford D'Amato. This is refreshing in its presentation and on the palate.

SANFORD RESTAURANT
1547 North Jackson
Milwaukee, Wisconsin

To make tabbouleh, heat 1½ tablespoons olive oil in medium sauté pan until hot. Add onions; sauté until transparent, about 2 minutes. Add rice and sauté for 30 seconds. Add hot chicken stock and bay leaf. Bring to a boil; cover with buttered parchment paper.

Place in a preheated 350° oven for 5 to 7 minutes or until liquid is absorbed. Remove bay leaf. Transfer to bowl; refrigerate. Core and score (on opposite side) tomatoes. Plunge into boiling water for 17 seconds. Put in ice water and peel, seed and finely dice. Add to cooled rice with remaining ingredients. Let stand at room temperature for at least 2 hours.

Combine all vinaigrette ingredients (except chives and mint) with whisk in small bowl. Set aside.

Dust grouper cheeks in flour seasoned with salt and pepper. Sauté in large sauté pan in hot olive oil until golden brown about 8 minutes. Place on bed of tabbouleh, spoon the tomato vinaigrette over and garnish with mint and chives. Serve with zucchini and yellow squash fans.

Swordfish
in Sun-Dried Tomato Vinaigrette

makes 6 servings

2 cups olive oil
¾ cup Balsamic vinegar
1 small onion, diced, about ¼ cup
2 cloves garlic, minced
1 teaspoon dried leaf oregano
½ teaspoon dried leaf basil
½ teaspoon dried leaf thyme
½ cup sun-dried tomatoes, cut in strips
1 teaspoon freshly ground black pepper
1½ teaspoons salt
6 swordfish* steaks (6-8 ounces *each*), 1 inch thick

Grilled swordfish is an unexpected pleasure. Team it with a marinade of olive oil, balsamic vinegar, herbs and sun-dried tomatoes for an intensely flavorful main dish.

In a food processor bowl fitted with a metal blade, process olive oil for 30 seconds. With processor running, add vinegar in a slow steady stream until all vinegar is incorporated. Add onion, garlic, oregano, basil, thyme, tomatoes, pepper and salt and process for 1 minute. Set aside.

Place steaks in a shallow non-aluminum dish. Cover completely with marinade. Cover dish with plastic wrap and refrigerate 6 hours or overnight.

Remove steaks from marinade and reserve. Grill fish over charcoal or gas grill (may also broil) over high heat until done, about 4 minutes per side. Fish should be opaque throughout.

Heat reserved marinade in small saucepan over medium heat until mixture comes to a boil and boil for 3 minutes. Drizzle over grilled steaks. Serve immediately.

* *You can use other fish such as shark, tuna or marlin.*

CARVERS ON THE LAKE RESTAURANT AND INN
N5529 County Trunk A
Green Lake, Wisconsin

Fresh Lake Superior Whitefish
with Beer, Capers and Julienne of Vegetables

makes 6 servings

6 fillets of fresh whitefish (8-10 ounces *each*), pinbones removed
3 tablespoons Dijon-style mustard (divided)
1 cup fresh white bread crumbs
1 bottle (12 ounces) Miller Genuine Draft Beer
½ pound unsalted butter, plus 2 tablespoons (can use margarine or vegetable oil) (divided)
2 tablespoons flour
⅛ teaspoon salt
2 tablespoons fresh lemon juice or to taste
⅓ cup julienne of leek
⅓ cup julienne of carrots
⅓ cup julienne of celery
36 capers

Chef Knut F. Apitz pays tribute to the good things of Wisconsin in this fresh whitefish entree sauced with some of Milwaukee's finest brew. A beautiful trio of julienne vegetables and a few capers make this dish a pleasure at the table.

Lay whitefish out on plastic or glass cutting surface and brush both sides with mustard. Coat with bread crumbs. Heat ½ pound of butter in large skillet or sauté pan over medium/high heat and sauté the white-fish until golden brown on both sides, about 3 minutes each side. Place fillets on paper towel to drain. Keep hot; set aside.

In a medium non-reactive saucepan, bring beer slowly to simmer over low heat. While beer heats make a beurre manie (hand butter) of 2 tablespoons remaining butter and 2 tablespoons flour, mixed together with your hands in a small bowl. Whisk beurre manie into beer to obtain desired sauce consistency (begin with 1 tablespoon beurre manie).

Flavor sauce with remaining 1 table-spoon mustard, salt and lemon juice. Stir in julienne vegetables and add capers, stir gently to blend. Lay out sauce thinly on 6 serving plates and place dry, hot fish fillets on top. Garnish around plate with addi-tional capers.

GRENADIER'S RESTAURANT
747 North Broadway at Mason
Milwaukee, Wisconsin

Brittany Baked Cod

makes 4 servings

Seasoning Paste:

¼ cup olive oil
⅓ large fennel bulb, about 2 ounces
1 small white onion
¼ cup fresh garlic cloves, peeled

Cod:

4 cod fillets (6 ounces *each*)
3 cups milk
12 teaspoons butter, clarified* (divided)

White Sauce:

¼ cup butter
¼ cup flour
1½ teaspoons freshly ground black pepper
¾ teaspoon salt
2 cups 2% milk

Roasted Vegetables:

4 medium russet potatoes, scrubbed, peeled and cut lengthwise in 8 wedges
4 large carrots, peeled, cut diagonally into 1½-inch pieces
1 fennel bulb, sliced ¼-thick
1 red onion, cut in ¼-inch thick wedges
2 leeks, cut diagonally in 1½ inch pieces (can use a bit of the green stalk)
Lemon wedges—garnish
4 sprigs of fresh thyme

Milwaukee Journal *restaurant critic, Dennis Getto, was impressed with this flavorful fish entree during his visits to Susie's Restaurant. Healthful and beautiful, this recipe is a "keeper". Owner Susie Quiriconi was happy to share her mother's treasured recipe from her files.*

Make seasoning paste by combining oil, fennel bulb, onion and garlic cloves in food processor or blender. Process until well-combined. Set aside.

In a 13" x 9" x 2" glass baking pan, stir together 3 tablespoons of seasoning paste with 3 cups milk until blended. (Leftover paste may be refrigerated and used with butter or margarine to season other baked fish or seafood.) Dip fillets in mixture, moistening both sides. Lay flat in pan and set aside.

SUSIE'S RESTAURANT
146 Fourth Avenue
Baraboo, Wisconsin

*Make clarified butter by melting 12 teaspoons butter in small saucepan over low heat. When completely melted, remove from heat, let stand for about 5 minutes allowing milk solids to settle to the bottom. Skim the foamy white butterfat from the top; discard. Spoon off the remaining clear yellow liquid—this is the clarified butter needed for this recipe, about 10 teaspoons.

Spoon 4 teaspoons clarified butter over fillets. Microwave on high for 2 minutes. Set aside.

Make white sauce by melting butter in heavy medium saucepan; whisk in flour, pepper and salt and cook for 2 minutes, whisking constantly. Add milk gradually and cook until slightly thickened, about 4 minutes. Set aside.

Place prepared vegetables in foil and parchment-lined roasting pan and drizzle with remaining 6 teaspoons clarified butter; stir to coat vegetables with butter. Roast at 500° for 20 minutes; stir vegetables. Place fish in 500° oven in separate baking pan and roast along side vegetables for 10 minutes. Vegetables should be golden brown and tender after 30 minutes total roasting time.

Remove fish fillets from milk mixture (curdling of milk is normal) to 4 serving plates and place ¼ of roasted vegetables on each plate. Pour ½ cup White Sauce over all and garnish with fresh lemon and thyme.

Pan-Fried Walleye
with Tomato Cumin Butter Sauce with Cilantro
makes 4 servings

Sauce:

½ cup white wine
¼ cup fresh lemon juice
1 teaspoon chili powder
1½ teaspoons cumin (divided)
1 teaspoon ground coriander
2 bunches of cilantro, washed,
  stemmed and chopped
  (divided), about 2 cups
½ cup heavy whipping cream
16 tablespoons salted butter

Walleye:

4 fillets of walleye (6-8 ounces
  each), pin-bone removed
½ cup vegetable oil
1 cup blue cornmeal flour
⅛ teaspoon cayenne pepper or to
  taste
½ teaspoon sea salt
¼ teaspoon white pepper
2 cups diced fresh tomatoes
4 jalapeno peppers, seeded and
  finely diced*

CAFE KNICKERBOCKER
*1030 East Juneau Avenue
Milwaukee, Wisconsin*

*Blue cornmeal shows up more fre-
quently on the West Coast and in the
Southwest than it does in the heartland,
but adventurous cooks will enjoy this
complex flavor mix from Chef Rob
Wagner that tantalizes and satisfies the
taste buds. Look for blue cornmeal at
specialty markets or at health food
stores.*

In a heavy 2-quart saucepan, place white
wine, lemon juice, chili powder, 1 teaspoon
cumin, coriander and half of chopped cilantro. Cook over medium/high heat reducing
volume by three-fourths.

Add cream and reduce by three-fourths
or cook until cream has thickened, stirring
occasionally. Over very low heat, slowly add
butter, one tablespoon at a time, stirring
constantly, until all butter has melted.

Bring mixture back to simmer, slowly,
stirring occasionally. Place saucepan in
larger container of warm water (110-120°) to
hold sauce until time to serve fish. Stir
occasionally.

Heat oil in large sauté pan or skillet over
medium heat for 2 minutes. Meanwhile
dredge walleye in cornmeal flour that is
seasoned with remaining ½ teaspoon
cumin, cayenne, salt and white pepper.

Place fillets in hot sauté pan, flesh side down and fry until crispy, about 4 minutes. Flip to skin side; fry for 3 minutes. Place on cookie sheet in preheated 400° oven for 5-10 minutes or until fish flakes easily.

To serve place each walleye portion on warm plate. Ladle sauce over walleye. Garnish each serving with ¼ each of diced tomato, jalapeno peppers and remaining cilantro.

* *When handling hot peppers, wear gloves and avoid contact with eyes and face. Wash hands thoroughly after handling.*

Lemon Dill Walleye Salad Sandwich

makes 8 sandwiches

4 walleye fillets (10-12 ounces
  each)
1 cup dry white wine
1 lemon, washed, sliced
  crosswise ⅛-inch thick
4 sprigs fresh dill
8 ounces cream cheese, softened
2 tablespoons sweet pickle
  relish
¼ cup minced red bell pepper
1 stalk celery, minced
1 teaspoon horseradish
½ cup mayonnaise
½ cup dairy sour cream
2 teaspoons capers, drained,
  minced
Dash hot pepper sauce
Dash Worcestershire sauce
¼ teaspoon salt
¼ teaspoon freshly ground black
  pepper
16 bibb lettuce leaves, washed
  and chilled
16 slices whole grain bread

*This delicately seasoned salad of flaky
pieces of walleye team exquisitely with
a few well-chosen vegetables and flavor-
ings from River Wildlife managed by
Aina Henegar. There is only one prob-
lem. Chef Mari Bayens' salad is so tasty
you may be tempted to eat it sans bread.*

In a large skillet or sauté pan, poach
walleye fillets in mixture of white wine,
fresh lemon slices and dill sprigs until fish
flakes easily with fork, 6-8 minutes. Remove
fish; drain well and discard cooking liquid.
When fish is cool, remove skin (discard) and
flake fish with fork. Set aside.

In a medium mixing bowl with electric
mixer on low speed, blend together cream
cheese, pickle relish, red pepper, celery,
horseradish, mayonnaise, sour cream,
capers, hot pepper, Worcestershire sauce
and salt and pepper. Gently fold in flaked
fish with wooden spoon.

Make sandwiches using whole grain
bread topped with lettuce leaves and salad
filling. Serve immediately; chill leftovers.

RIVER WILDLIFE
Kohler, Wisconsin

Scallops and Andouille Sausage
with Lemon Linguine

makes 4 servings

½ cup olive oil
1 medium red bell pepper (4
  ounces), cut in julienne strips
1 medium green bell pepper (4
  ounces), cut in julienne strips
2 teaspoons minced garlic
16 large sea scallops, fresh or
  frozen, thawed
8 ounces andouille sausage,
  cooked, sliced ¼-inch thick
1½ cups white wine
8 teaspoons fresh lemon juice
½ cup fresh minced parsley
8 ounces lemon linguine, cooked
  and drained

*A quick and pretty pasta main dish
that relies on a mixture of multi-colored
bell peppers and the juxtaposition of
mild scallops and spicy andouille for its
distinguished flavors.*

In a 10-inch diameter skillet or sauté pan,
heat olive oil over medium/high heat until
hot. Sauté red and green peppers and garlic
in olive oil about 1 minute. Add scallops,
sauté, stirring constantly, for 1 minute.

Add sausage, wine, lemon juice and
parsley. Cook for 1 minute. Serve over hot
lemon linguine.

THE RESTAURANT
*1800 North Point Drive
Stevens Point, Wisconsin*

Shrimp and Artichoke Romano

makes 4 servings

8 ounces uncooked linguine
14 tablespoons unsalted butter,
  clarified* (divided)
16 jumbo or large shrimp (18-20
  ounces), peeled and deveined
8 canned artichoke hearts,
  drained, cut in half lengthwise
2 tablespoons minced garlic
1 teaspoon salt
½ teaspoon freshly ground black
  pepper
1 cup dry white wine
¾ cup grated Romano cheese
4 teaspoons chopped fresh
  parsley

THE WHITE GULL INN
4225 Main Street
Fish Creek, Wisconsin

Soft pinks and greens combine with linguine for a picture pretty pasta dish. This recipe calls for clarified butter which is easily made and reduces the chances of burning the butter during the sautéing process.

*This recipe uses clarified butter (butter from which milk solids have been removed which allows the butter to be heated to higher temperatures without burning). To make clarified butter, melt 6 tablespoons butter in small saucepan over low heat. When completely melted, remove from heat, let stand for about 5 minutes allowing the milk solids to settle to the bottom. Skim the foamy white butterfat from the top; discard. Spoon off the clear yellow liquid and reserve—this is the clarified butter. Set aside. Discard the milk solids on the bottom of the pan. You should have approximately 5 tablespoons clarified butter for pan sautéing.

Cook linguine in large kettle of boiling water (at least 4 quarts), about 7 minutes for dried linguine or 3 minutes for fresh linguine, to stage that it is pleasant "to the tooth" al dente—firm yet tender. Drain well in colander; set aside.

In a 10-inch diameter skillet, heat 5 tablespoons clarified butter and sauté shrimp and artichoke hearts for 3-4 minutes or until shrimp is opaque and almost cooked through. Add garlic, salt and pepper and cook until garlic browns just slightly, about 20 seconds.

Add white wine and cheese and simmer over low heat until liquid is slightly thickened, approximately 30 seconds. Reduce heat; add 8 remaining tablespoons butter (room temperature), one tablespoon at a time, whisking constantly. *Do not let the sauce boil.* Sauce should cook until the consistency of heavy cream.

Toss in cooked linguine, stir together to heat and evenly distribute ingredients. Sprinkle with parsley. Serve immediately.

Seafood Fettuccine

makes 4 servings

4 tablespoons unsalted butter
2 teaspoons fresh crushed garlic
4 tablespoons finely chopped
  onions
12 ounces small peeled and
  deveined shrimp
12 ounces small bay scallops
¼ cup Chablis wine
2 teaspoons freshly squeezed
  lemon juice
1 cup dairy sour cream
½ cup freshly grated Parmesan
  cheese (divided)
¼ cup heavy whipping cream
1 pound fettuccine noodles,
  cooked and well-drained
½ teaspoon salt or to taste
½ teaspoon freshly ground black
  pepper
Fresh parsley sprigs—garnish
2 lemon wedges—garnish

Pasta and seafood pair up in this pretty dish that goes together quickly (less than 30 minutes) but leaves the cook unharried and presents a soft palette of pink and cream with every serving.

In a 10-inch diameter skillet or sauté pan, melt butter over medium heat. Add garlic, onions, shrimp and scallops. Sauté lightly, about 2-3 minutes, being careful not to over-cook.

Add wine and lemon juice; cook over medium heat until liquid thickens slightly, about 2 minutes. Add sour cream, 4 table-spoons Parmesan cheese and heavy cream.

Stir in pasta, salt and pepper, mixing to blend. Heat over medium heat until warmed through. Serve on a hot plate garnished with parsley and lemon wedges and remaining 4 tablespoons Parmesan cheese, if desired.

**NORTON'S
MARINE DINING ROOM**
*South Lawson Drive
Green Lake, Wisconsin*

MEATS

Grilled Smoked Pork Chops
with Maple Corn Relish

makes 4 servings

1½ cups fresh or frozen corn,
   cooked
¼ cup finely diced yellow onion
2 tablespoons finely diced sweet
   green pepper
2 tablespoons finely diced sweet
   red pepper
½ cup maple syrup (divided)
¼ cup cider vinegar
1 teaspoon leaf thyme, crumbled
½ teaspoon salt
¼ teaspoon freshly ground black
   pepper
4 smoked pork chops (8 ounces
   each), 1-inch thick

Here's a recipe for the grill that's quick and easy and makes an attractive presentation. Smoked pork chops are precooked so they require just minimal time to grill, lightly brushed with maple syrup. Do make the corn relish as it is tasty and colorful.

Make maple corn relish by combining corn, onion, peppers, ¼ cup maple syrup, vinegar, thyme, salt and pepper in medium bowl. Set aside to blend flavors at room temperature for at least one hour.

Prepare grill with hot coals or have gas grill set to high. Brush pork chops with remaining ¼ cup maple syrup; grill 2 minutes on each side, basting with syrup as desired.

Serve each chop with one-fourth of relish on the side.

THE VINTAGE
3110 8th Street South
Wisconsin Rapids, Wisconsin

Pork Tenderloin
with Wisconsin Cranberry Sauce

makes 4 servings

Sauce:

1 large greening apple
¼ cup white wine
1 bag (12 ounces) cranberries
½ cup water
½ teaspoon grated lemon zest
⅛ teaspoon ground cinnamon
¾ cup sugar

Tenderloin:

3 pounds pork tenderloin
¼ cup flour
6 tablespoons unsalted butter
½ cup red wine
½ cup brown sauce (Espagnole)
¼ teaspoon salt
⅛ teaspoon freshly ground black
   pepper

All the favorite flavors of Wisconsin comingle in this dish that features lean and tender pork tenderloin. Check the Chef's Helper for information on Espagnole.

Peel and core the apple, cutting into ¼-inch thick slices. Steam apple slices in small saucepan with wine over medium heat until tender, about 5 minutes. Do not overcook. Set aside.

In a small saucepan, place cranberries, water, lemon zest and cinnamon. Cover; simmer at low heat for 10 minutes. Stir in sugar until blended. Press through a fine sieve to remove seeds and skins. This should yield 1 cup sauce.

Trim pork tenderloin of any fat and remove silver skins. Cut into 6 steaks, butterfly each and pound to ¼-inch thickness. Dredge fillets in flour. Set aside.

In a large 12-inch diameter skillet, heat butter and sauté steaks at low temperature until cooked through. Do not overcook. Remove steaks to a warm platter; cover to retain warmth.

Deglaze skillet with red wine, scraping up any browned bits from pan surface. Add brown sauce and cranberry sauce and bring to a simmer. Add salt and pepper. Pour sauce over pork tenderloin steaks and garnish with steamed apple slices. Serve with baby carrots and small red potatoes.

BERNARD'S *Encore*
701 Second Street North
Stevens Point, Wisconsin

Beef Fillets
with Green Peppercorn Roquefort Sauce

makes 4 servings

Fillets:

8 beef tenderloin medallions (3 ounces each), about 1-inch thick
1 teaspoon salt (divided)
½ teaspoon freshly ground black pepper

Sauce:

¼ cup finely diced onions
1 tablespoon finely chopped garlic
½ cup sherry
1 tablespoon Worcestershire sauce
2 tablespoons Dijon-style mustard
1 cup beef broth
¼ cup green peppercorns, drained
3 ounces crumbled Roquefort cheese
½ cup dairy sour cream

If you have never paired beef with Roquefort cheese, here's a nice recipe with minimal difficulty that has tangy green peppercorns for an extra flavor fillip.

Sprinkle medallions with ½ teaspoon salt and pepper; pound lightly on both sides until medallions are less than ½-inch thick.

Heat a 9-inch well-seasoned cast iron skillet over high heat until hot, about 2-3 minutes. Sear medallions on both sides in skillet until brown on surface, about 1 minute per side. Do not overcrowd. Reduce heat and cook until desired doneness, about 3 minutes for medium rare. Remove medallions from pan, arrange on warmed serving platter, covering meat with foil.

Using same skillet, sauté onions and garlic in pan juices until transparent, about 1 minute. Add sherry and deglaze by heating over medium/high heat, scraping loose the browned bits on bottom of pan.

Add Worcestershire sauce, mustard, broth, peppercorns, cheese and remaining ½ teaspoon salt, if desired. Reduce heat to low and stir until cheese is melted. Add sour cream and reduce until sauce is consistency of heavy cream. Ladle sauce over beef medallions.

THE VINTAGE
3110 8th Street South
Wisconsin Rapids, Wisconsin

Beef Tenderloin Wrapped in Bacon
with Maple Vinegar Sauce
makes 2 servings

Maple Vinegar Sauce:

2 tablespoons unsalted butter
2 tablespoons chopped onion
4 tablespoons maple syrup
¼ cup red wine vinegar or apple
  cider vinegar
1 teaspoon liquid smoke
4 medallions of beef tenderloin
  (4 ounces *each*)
4 slices of lean bacon
2 teaspoons Worcestershire
  sauce

A quick beef tenderloin entree from Sous Chef Boyd Thew that stays pleasantly uncomplicated yet is delightfully piquant with its maple vinegar sauce.

In a small skillet or sauté pan, melt butter and sauté onions until transparent. Add syrup, vinegar and liquid smoke; stir to blend. Keep warm—do not thicken.

Wrap each medallion with a strip of bacon, securing with wooden pick, if necessary. Brush with Worcestershire sauce on each side. Broil or charcoal grill medallions 3-4 minutes on each side for medium rare. Top with warm sauce.

RED CIRCLE INN
Encore
N44 W33013 Watertown Plank Road
Nashotah, Wisconsin

Sicilian Breaded Steak
with Garlic Sauce

makes 4 generous servings

Sauce:

10 tablespoons reconstituted
   lemon juice (divided)
2 cloves garlic, finely diced
¼ teaspoon finely ground pepper
⅜ teaspoon salt
¾ teaspoon dried leaf oregano
¼ cup vegetable oil
2 tablespoons water

Breaded Steak:

1 cup fine dry bread crumbs
2¼ teaspoons dried leaf basil
3 tablespoons grated Romano
   cheese
¾ teaspoon salt
¾ teaspoon freshly ground black
   pepper
¼ cup butter, softened
4 New York strip, T-bone, or rib
   eye steaks (12 ounces *each*)

THE GRANARY
50 West 6th Street
Oshkosh, Wisconsin

A tasty light breading combines with a zesty garlic sauce to add interest to any tender steak of your choice. Leftover garlic sauce can be brushed on a variety of other meats, poultry and fish.

To make garlic sauce, in small blender container place 1 tablespoon lemon juice and diced garlic. Blend thoroughly to liquify garlic. Add remaining 9 tablespoons lemon juice, pepper, salt and oregano. Blend for 30 seconds. Add vegetable oil and water and blend to combine all ingredients. Store, covered, in refrigerator and use to brush over steak, chicken, pork chops, swordfish, red snapper and yellow fin tuna during broiling. (Sauce will become more flavorful as it ages.)

In a medium bowl, combine bread crumbs, basil, cheese, ¾ teaspoon salt and ¾ teaspoon black pepper. Set aside.

Spread softened butter on steaks in a thin layer using a serrated knife. Coat both sides of steak with seasoned bread crumb mixture.

Broil 4 inches from heat in preheated broiler, about 6 minutes on each side for medium, brushing both sides of steak with garlic sauce halfway through broiling. Serve immediately.

Guinness Brisket

makes 10 servings

5 pounds beef brisket
1 can beef consomme (10½ ounces)
¾ cup water
1 bottle Guinness Stout (12 ounces)
1 cup chopped tomato
½ cup chopped celery
½ cup chopped carrots
½ cup chopped onion
1 teaspoon chopped garlic
1 bay leaf
3 whole black peppercorns
¼ cup flour
5 tablespoons butter, clarified*

The hearty flavor of Guinness Stout seeps into this tasty slowly cooked brisket of beef created by Executive Chef Tim Gurtner. This would be a fine choice for a Super Bowl Party—and serve with Colcannon, page 66. Beer makes a fine accompaniment.

In a 4½-quart kettle, place brisket, consomme, water, stout, tomato, celery, carrots, onion, garlic, bay leaf and peppercorns. Bring to a simmer, cover and cook for 3½ to 4 hours or until meat is fork tender.

*To clarify butter, melt in small saucepan over low heat. When completely melted, remove from heat; let stand for about 5 minutes allowing the milk solids to settle to the bottom. Skim the foamy white butterfat from the top; discard. Spoon off the clear yellow liquid—this is the 4 tablespoons clarified butter needed for the roux.

Carefully remove brisket; cool on platter. Strain stock, discarding vegetables and herbs. Let stock rest for 5 minutes. Skim grease from stock; return to a clean saucepan over medium heat and continue cooking.

Make a roux by whisking together flour and butter in heavy saucepan over low heat, stirring frequently. Cook for 3-4 minutes. Add roux to hot stock and whisk until sauce is thickened. Set aside.

Trim excess fat from brisket and slice into ½-inch thick slices across the grain. Add sliced brisket to warm sauce and serve with Colcannon.

52 STAFFORD
Encore
52 Stafford Street
Plymouth, Wisconsin

Lamb Spring Green

makes 8 servings

Stock:

2 pounds lamb bones
½ cup coarsely chopped onion
½ cup coarsely chopped celery
½ cup coarsely chopped carrots
1 bay leaf
8 whole black peppercorns
1 tablespoon tomato paste

Lamb:

2 racks of lamb (about 1½
   pounds *each* or 7-8 ribs *each*,
   Frenched*)
1 large pork tenderloin (about 1
   pound)
⅛ teaspoon dried leaf rosemary,
   crumbled
1¼ teaspoons chopped garlic
   (divided)
⅛ teaspoon dried leaf basil
⅛ teaspoon dried dill weed
½ teaspoon salt (divided)
½ teaspoon freshly ground black
   pepper (divided)
1½ teaspoons extra-virgin olive
   oil (divided)
2 cups heavy whipping cream

CHRISTIE'S
333 West College Avenue
Appleton, Wisconsin

If you love lamb, make this festive special occasion entree. Much of the work is done by your butcher as the recipe specifies. You will end up with a herb-flavored boneless loin of lamb wrapped in a butterflied pork loin, quick-roasted to perfection. The rosemary-tinged sauce is a delight—a creation from Executive Chef Chuck Schuster and Sous Chef Terry Rathsack.

Remove lamb rack bones (use in lamb stock) and fat cap from lamb rack making a horizontal cut along top of loin. You now should have a boneless eye of lamb loin. Set aside.

Make a stock by combining 2 pounds lamb bones, enough water to cover, onion, celery, carrot, bay leaf, peppercorns and tomato paste in 13" x 9" x 2" baking pan. Roast in preheated 350° oven for 1 hour. Pour into large deep saucepan and simmer for 1½ hours on low. Drain off vegetables, spices and reserve broth (stock). You should have 2 cups stock.

Make garlic sauce by reducing lamb stock to ¼ cup in saucepan over medium/high heat. Add 1 teaspoon chopped garlic and whipping cream. Reduce until sauce coats the back of a spoon and yields about 1 cup, 10 minutes. Season as desired with salt and pepper. Keep warm; set aside.

Season reserved lamb loin with rosemary, ¼ teaspoon salt and ¼ teaspoon pepper and sear on all sides in ¾ teaspoon olive oil over high heat in sauté pan. Remove from pan and refrigerate, covered.

Remove silver skin from pork tenderloin. Cut pork tenderloin about 2-inches longer than lamb loin. Split pork tenderloin lengthwise to butterfly. Place tenderloin between a sheet of plastic wrap and flatten to about ⅛-inch thickness. Remove plastic wrap. Season with remaining ¼ teaspoon chopped garlic, basil, dill, remaining ¼ teaspoon salt, and remaining ¼ teaspoon pepper.

Place seared lamb loin in center of pork tenderloin. Fold side of pork over lamb and roll tight. Secure at intervals with wooden picks, or plain dental floss, if desired. Heat remaining ¾ teaspoon olive oil in sauté pan and sear stuffed pork tenderloin until brown.

Bake in preheated 500° for 15 minutes or until internal temperature reaches 130°. Remove from pan and let rest on cutting surface for 10 minutes.

Cut meat into ¼-inch thick slices. Place four slices in fan pattern on plate with sauce in center of plate.

* *Frenched refers to removal of excess fat and scrap meat on top edge of ribs. Be sure to have the butcher remove the chine bones (backbone) from the rack for easier carving. Ask butcher for lamb bones to make stock.*

Veal Strips
with Peppers
makes 4 servings

1 pound veal, cut from round,
   sliced into strips 2-inches long
   by ¼-inch wide
3 tablespoons butter, clarified*
1-2 teaspoons minced garlic
2 ounces sherry
1 pint heavy whipping cream
1 red bell pepper, cut in julienne
   strips
1 green bell pepper, cut in
   julienne strips
1 yellow bell pepper, cut in
   julienne strips
1 teaspoon salt
¼ teaspoon freshly ground black
   pepper
¾ pound cooked linguine,
   drained
Freshly grated nutmeg—garnish
Freshly grated Parmesan
   cheese—garnish

**THE CREAMERY
RESTAURANT AND INN**
*County Trunk C
Downsville, Wisconsin*

Sweet bell peppers with their bright colors make most any dish come alive. Try this veal entree delicately sauced and dusted with nutmeg and fresh Parmesan cheese. A favorite of the Thomas Brothers, owners of the Creamery.

*To clarify butter, melt 3 tablespoons butter in small saucepan over low heat. Let stand for about 5 minutes allowing the milk solids to settle to the bottom. Skim the foamy white butterfat from the top; discard. Spoon off the clear yellow liquid—this is the clarified butter needed for this recipe, about 2 tablespoons.

In a 9-inch diameter skillet or sauté pan, sauté veal strips in hot clarified butter, turning once, until browned and cooked, about 4 minutes. Remove veal from pan and reserve, keeping strips warm. Reduce heat to medium.

Sauté garlic for 10 seconds, stirring constantly. Stir in sherry and cream; reduce mixture by half, about 10 minutes. Add bell peppers and continue reducing mixture until the consistency of a sauce, about 10 minutes. Stir veal strips into sauce. Season with salt and pepper.

Serve over linguine. Garnish with Parmesan cheese and nutmeg. Serve with a rich Chardonnay.

Provimi Veal Scallopini Mediterranean

makes 4 servings

½ cup unsalted butter, clarified*
16 slices of Provimi veal inside
  round (1 ounce *each*)
½ cup flour
2 teaspoons finely chopped
  garlic
1 cup dry white wine
8 ounces sliced black olives
4 ounces capers, drained
2 cups canned diced tomatoes
  with juice
Lemon zest or chive—garnish

All the colors and flavors of the Mediterranean complement this beautiful, quick and easy veal entree—an ideal entree for carefree entertaining from Chef Peter Baldus.

*To make clarified butter for this recipe, melt ½ cup butter in small saucepan over low heat. When completely melted, remove from heat, let stand for about 5 minutes allowing the milk solids to settle to the bottom. Skim the foamy white butterfat from the top; discard. Spoon off the clear yellow liquid—this is the clarified butter needed for this recipe, about 7 tablespoons. Set aside. Discard the milk solids on the bottom of the pan.

Using the side of a meat cleaver or meat mallet, lightly pound the veal slices enough to break the marbling. Dredge lightly in flour; set aside.

In a sauté pan or large skillet over medium heat, heat about 7 tablespoons clarified butter, about 1 minute. Add veal to pan (do not overcrowd) and sauté 1 minute on first side. Turn veal and add garlic, white wine, olives, capers, tomatoes, and juice. Cook 2 minutes on second side.

Place four slices each on warm serving plate with sauce and garnish with lemon zest or chives.

RED CIRCLE INN
Encore
N44 W33013 Watertown Plank Road
Nashotah, Wisconsin

Venison Geschnetzlte

makes 8 servings

2 pounds venison steak, cut
  ¼-inch thick
2 tablespoons unsalted butter
½ cup finely chopped onion
8 ounces fresh mushrooms,
  cleaned and sliced crosswise
½ cup dry white wine, Chablis
  preferred
1½ tablespoons flour
1 teaspoon salt
½ teaspoon freshly ground black
  pepper
½ cup dairy sour cream
2 tablespoons chopped fresh
  parsley

*Wisconsin cooks search for new ways
to cook venison. Here's a delicious
recipe from Eva-Maria Coughlin that is
reminiscent of the flavors of Stroganoff.
We used venison tenderloins provided
by a friend and found it wonderful.*

Slice the venison steaks into strips 2″ x
½″ x ¼″ thick; set aside. Melt butter in
9-inch diameter skillet and add venison
strips, browning strips on all sides.

Stir in onion and mushrooms; sauté,
stirring constantly for 5 minutes. Add white
wine and simmer for 2 minutes. Sprinkle
flour, salt and pepper over mixture and
whisk into liquid; let cook for 1 minute.
Reduce heat to low; gently stir in sour
cream. *Do not let boil.* Sprinkle with
parsley and serve over spaetzle.

CAFE MOZART
311 West Main Street
Durand, Wisconsin

FOR GOOD MEASURE

Cherry Chutney

makes 4 cups

2¼ pounds pre-sweetened tart
  cherries
½ cup diced green bell pepper
½ cup diced onion
1¼ cups brown sugar or more to
  taste
1 cup apple cider vinegar
¼ teaspoon ground allspice
¼ teaspoon ground cloves
¼ cup raisins

Chutneys are enjoying a revival of popularity and much of it has to do with the interesting fruit, vegetable and sweet spice combinations chefs create. Try this Door County favorite used with stuffed roasted pork loin.

In a 3½-quart heavy kettle, combine cherries, green pepper, onion, brown sugar and vinegar. Bring to a boil over medium/high heat. Reduce heat to low and let simmer, uncovered, until mixture starts to thicken, about 1 hour.

Stir in allspice, cloves and raisins; let simmer 30 minutes longer. Remove from heat. Pack into sterilized jars; cover tightly. Store refrigerated between uses. The Inn uses this as a topping for their cherry stuffed roasted pork loin.

THE INN AT CEDAR CROSSING
336 Louisiana Street
Sturgeon Bay, Wisconsin

Chunky Tomato Relish

makes 5 cups

3 cans whole tomatoes (28
  ounces *each*) drained, juice
  reserved (divided)
1 tablespoon corn oil
1 tablespoon olive oil
2 large cloves garlic, crushed
½ cup plus 2 tablespoons minced
  fresh parsley
2 tablespoons dried leaf basil or
  ⅓ cup fresh minced basil
½ teaspoon salt or to taste
¼ teaspoon freshly ground black
  pepper

*Don't even hesitate to make this ac-
companiment from the talented team of
Christy and Craig. It goes together
quickly and if you don't use it all in the
Ratatouille, recipe on page 70, you'll
find it garnishes black bean dishes and
tops Boboli pizza crusts to perfection.*

Dice drained tomatoes to size of large
kernel corn; set aside. Heat oil in large
skillet or sauté pan. Add one-half of tomatoes and garlic; sauté for 2-3 minutes,
adding 1 cup of reserved juice during last
minute of cooking. Refrigerate remaining
juice for future use.

Cook over medium heat until most of
liquid has boiled off, about 25 minutes.
Remove and discard garlic. Add remaining
tomatoes, parsley, basil and salt and pepper.
Cover tightly and refrigerate.

WILSON STREET GRILL
217 South Hamilton
Madison, Wisconsin

Tropical Salsa
for Blackened or Grilled Fish

makes 4 cups

1 small mango, peeled and diced
1 small papaya, peeled and diced
½ large red onion, diced
1 medium red bell pepper, diced
2 fresh kiwi, peeled and mashed
    with a fork
2 tablespoons sugar
2 tablespoons orange juice
2 tablespoons fresh lime juice
2 tablespoons Triple Sec liqueur
2 tablespoons balsamic vinegar
½ teaspoon salt
¼ teaspoon freshly ground black
    pepper
2 cloves fresh garlic minced
1 bunch fresh cilantro, stemmed,
    leaves minced
3 tablespoons olive or vegetable
    oil

Colorful fresh fruit and vegetable salsas are replacing many of the heavier sauces of recent memory. Here's a beautiful one from Chef Peter Jennings to use with any blackened or grilled fish.

In a large glass or stainless steel bowl, combine mango, papaya, onion and red bell pepper. Set aside. Combine mashed kiwi and sugar well; add to fruit and vegetable mixture. Stir in orange and lime juice, Triple Sec, balsamic vinegar, salt, pepper, garlic and cilantro.

Slowly whisk in oil in a thin stream to create an emulsion.

THE VINTAGE
3110 8th Street South
Wisconsin Rapids, Wisconsin

Herb Butter

makes about 3/4 pound

¾ pound unsalted butter, room
   temperature
1 tablespoon chopped fresh
   garlic
1 tablespoon chopped shallots
½ teaspoon minced fresh parsley
2 green onions, minced
2 tablespoons each of combined
   fresh minced dill, oregano and
   thyme
2 tablespoons Pernod liqueur

At the Sandhill Inn, this Herb Butter is used with their popular Poached Salmon entree, on page 99, and also served with their bread. Freeze it in tiny parcels and use with vegetables, too.

In a large mixing bowl with electric mixer, combine all ingredients on low speed until blended, about 4 minutes. Gradually increase the mixer speed allowing butter to increase in volume, about 5 minutes.

Remove the butter from bowl and place on a large sheet of waxed paper. Form butter into a roll in waxed paper and wrap tightly with plastic wrap. Freeze the roll and cut off sections as needed.

THE SANDHILL INN
170 East Main Street, Hwy. 78
Merrimac, Wisconsin

Veal Demi-Glace

makes about 6 cups

4 veal bones, knuckles split
2 veal shanks
2 large carrots, peeled, coarsely
   chopped
2 large onions, coarsely chopped
½ stalk of celery, coarsely
   chopped
1 can tomato paste (18 ounces)
2 tablespoons whole black
   peppercorns
1 quart brown sauce
   (Espagnole)*
1 quart unsalted veal stock
1 liter dry red wine
1 Bouquet garni of 3 sprigs each
   fresh rosemary, thyme,
   parsley

If you've never made a veal demi-glace before and like the idea of something aromatic and enticing simmering on the back burner for several days, then this recipe is for you. If not, take a shortcut and call your specialty market which sells their own glace, frozen for your convenience.

In a large roasting pan, place split veal bones and shanks and roast at 400° until dark brown, about 1 hour. Place carrots, onion and celery in pan with bones and shanks and continue roasting until vegetables are dark brown, about 1 hour. Remove from oven, reserving pan and juices for deglazing.

Place veal bones and vegetables in bottom of a heavy 10-quart stockpot, laying shanks on top. Add tomato paste, peppercorns and pour brown sauce and veal stock over mixture. Set aside.

Deglaze the roasting pan with red wine, scraping all browned bits and juices into wine. Pour into stock pot. If liquid does not cover bones, shanks and vegetables by at least 4 quarts, add enough water to reach that level. Bring mixture to boil over high heat; reduce to simmer. Let simmer on lowest heat, uncovered, for two days.

THE SANDHILL INN
170 East Main Street, Hwy. 78
Merrimac, Wisconsin

Carefully skim off fat that rises to top. Add water as necessary if liquid level gets too low. Do not allow to burn on the bottom. Strain liquid through fine sieve, reserving veal shanks for another meal, such as osso bucco.

Place strained liquid with bouquet garni in clean stockpot and reduce by one-half over medium heat, about 2 hours. Re-strain sauce. Chill to below 40° and then freeze small portions of sauce in ice cube trays, remove and wrap for freezer storage in heavy aluminum foil and use as needed.

* *If Espagnole (brown sauce) is not available, you could use a good quality brown gravy mix and add some additional veal bones to enrich the flavor.*

Court Bouillon

makes 3 quarts

8 cups cold water
3½ cups dry white wine
½ cup distilled vinegar
2 large white onions, coarsely
  chopped
2 large carrots, peeled and
  coarsely chopped
1 rib celery, washed and
  coarsely chopped
1 Bouquet garni of 1 sprig each
  fresh thyme and parsley
2 tablespoons salt
1 large lemon, washed, cut in
  half
½ teaspoon whole black
  peppercorns

Chef Paul J. Short III suggests that you make this poaching liquid for fresh fish and seafood in quantity and freeze, then use as needed.

In a large 4-5 quart kettle, combine all ingredients except peppercorns and simmer, covered, for 25 minutes. Add peppercorns and simmer for 10 more minutes. Strain through cheesecloth or fine sieve, discarding vegetables, herbs, spices and lemon halves. Court bouillon is now ready to use as a poaching medium for fish/seafood.

Refrigerate or freeze until time of use. This may be reused and refrozen between fish/seafood poaching.

THE SANDHILL INN
170 East Main Street, Hwy. 78
Merrimac, Wisconsin

DESSERTS

Encore

Cherry Nut Bread Pudding
with Cherry Sauce

makes 9 servings

Pudding:

1 cup sugar
4 large eggs
½ teaspoon salt
1½ teaspoons cinnamon
½ teaspoon nutmeg
3 cups milk
½ cup unsalted butter, melted
4 cups unsweetened* red tart
　cherries, packed in own
　juice (divided)
2 tablespoons flour
8 cups bread cubes, cut ¾-inch
　in size
½ cup chopped pecans or
　walnuts

Sauce:

Reserved 1⅓ cups cherries
　plus juice
¼ cup sugar or to taste
1 tablespoon cornstarch

THE WHITE GULL INN
4225 Main Street
Fish Creek, Wisconsin

If you've never met a bread pudding that you haven't liked, you will want to add this Door County version to your list of comfort desserts.

Combine first four ingredients in large mixing bowl; beat until well blended with mixer at medium speed for 1-2 minutes. Set aside.

Scald milk in small saucepan by bringing temperature to 180°. Melt butter by placing it in hot milk. Set aside.

Drain cherries from juice. Measure out 2⅔ cups cherries and toss them with flour. Reserve the remaining cherries and juice for cherry sauce. Combine cooled milk and butter with egg mixture in large bowl.

Place floured cherries, bread cubes and chopped nuts in a greased 8-inch square baking pan. Pour milk mixture over cherry layer (pan will be full). Place pan inside a larger baking dish containing 1-inch of water. Bake in preheated oven at 350° for 40-45 minutes.

Make cherry sauce by heating reserved 1 cup cherry juice, remaining ½ cup sugar and cornstarch in medium saucepan over medium high heat. Bring mixture to a boil; boil one minute, stirring constantly. Gently stir reserved cherries into thickened cherry sauce. Remove from heat. Serve over warm pudding.

* *If you use partially sweetened cherries, reduce the sugar in the pudding to ½ cup and reduce the sugar in the sauce to taste.*

Cranberry Sorbet

makes 4 quarts

3 cans (12 ounces each) frozen
 cranberry juice cocktail
 concentrate
1 can (12 ounces) frozen
 cranberry/apple juice cocktail
 concentrate
1 can (12 ounces) frozen
 lemonade concentrate
1 bottle (24 ounces) sparkling
 (non-alcoholic) white grape
 juice
1 tablespoon peeled, finely
 grated ginger root
Fresh mint sprigs—garnish
Fresh cranberries—garnish

This beautiful sorbet, infused with just enough fresh ginger, not only cleanses the palate between courses but refreshes our whole being. Keep this in mind if you have holiday guests who prefer something light and refreshing for a dessert course.

Combine ingredients in large mixing bowl to blend (will yield about 10 cups of liquid); chill until cold. If you have a 4-quart (or larger) ice cream maker, this can be made in 1 batch. If a smaller ice cream maker is used, divide mixture and make in batches.

Freeze sorbet mixture in ice cream maker according to manufacturer's directions. (Slower freezing will result in a smoother texture—follow ice cream maker instructions for slower freezing.) Package in freezer-proof plastic containers, seal and freeze at zero degrees or below for firm texture. When serving, garnish with mint sprigs and sliced cranberries.

THE OLD RITTENHOUSE INN
301 Rittenhouse Avenue
Bayfield, Wisconsin

Heath Bar Pie

makes 10 decadent servings

Crust:

1¼ cups unsalted butter (divided)
1 cup granulated sugar plus 6
    tablespoons (divided)
1 large egg
1½ teaspoons vanilla
⅛ teaspoon instant coffee
    crystals
2½ tablespoons cold water
1 cup flour plus 2 tablespoons
3 tablespoons cornstarch
6 tablespoons cocoa
¼ teaspoon salt
¼ teaspoon cream of tartar

Filling:

1 pound cream cheese, room
    temperature
1⅛ cups brown sugar
1 teaspoon cornstarch
1⅔ cups dairy sour cream
3 large eggs
3 egg yolks
2 teaspoons vanilla
2 teaspoons white rum
⅛ teaspoon salt
⅓ cup chopped pecans

Topping:

1¼ cups semisweet chocolate
    chips
½ cup heavy whipping cream

Toffee Crumbles:

(Makes enough for 4 pies)

2 cups unsalted butter
2 cups granulated sugar
¼ cup water
2 tablespoons maple syrup

This is one of the desserts that has made Susie's Restaurant famous—and one bite will tell you why. Creamy and rich, it is surprisingly balanced in its flavors. Extra Toffee Crumbles can be stored tightly covered and used with a hot fudge sauce on ice cream or eaten as candy.

SUSIE'S RESTAURANT
146 Fourth Avenue
Baraboo, Wisconsin

In large mixing bowl with electric mixer, cream together ¾ cup butter with 1 cup plus 2 tablespoons sugar until lightened, about 2-3 minutes. Beat in egg. Add vanilla and coffee crystals dissolved in water.

Whisk together in separate bowl, flour, cornstarch, cocoa, salt and cream of tartar; add to creamed mixture, blending well. Drop cookie batter from teaspoon onto greased baking sheet, 2 inches apart. Bake in preheated 350° oven for 8-10 minutes or until cookie springs back when lightly touched. Remove to cooling rack to cool completely.

Process cookies to a fine crumb in work bowl of food processor fitted with a metal blade. Combine crumbs with remaining 4 tablespoons granulated sugar and remaining ½ cup melted butter to make crust. Prepare a 10-inch diameter springform pan by lining the bottom with parchment paper. Spray the sides of pan with vegetable oil. Press crumbs onto sides and across bottom of prepared pan; set aside.

Cream cheese, brown sugar and cornstarch together in large mixing bowl with electric mixer until lightened. Add sour cream; blend. Whip in eggs, yolks, vanilla, rum and salt with electric mixer, until mixture is light and fluffy, about 5 minutes. (Longer mixing results in a lighter cheesecake.) Scrape down sides occasionally. Gently stir in pecans. Pour on top of crumb crust. Bake at 325° about 40 minutes—cheesecake should jiggle slightly in center. Cool in pan on wire rack; then refrigerate until cold.

Make ganache topping by placing chips in work bowl of food processor fitted with metal blade; process until in tiny particles. Bring cream to a boil; pour into chocolate while processing. Process until smooth. Remove cheesecake from pan; spread ganache over cold cheesecake.

Make toffee crumbles by melting butter over low heat in medium-heavy saucepan. Add sugar and stir. Stir until mixture reaches a full rolling boil, about 10 minutes. Add syrup and water; mix well. Stir occasionally and cook over low heat to 290° F. Pour onto lightly buttered pan; crumble when cool.

Cut pie into 10 servings. Sprinkle each piece with 2 tablespoons toffee crumbles. (Freeze remaining toffee crumbles in airtight container for future use.)

Kentucky Derby Pie

makes 8-10 servings

1 unbaked pie crust (9-inch),
   homemade or purchased
   refrigerated crust
½ cup unsalted butter
2 squares (1 ounce each)
   unsweetened chocolate
1½ cups sugar (divided)
4 large eggs (divided)
2 teaspoons vanilla (divided)
¾ cup flour
1½ cups chopped walnuts
   (divided)
1 cup light corn syrup

This luscious pie will bring chocolate lovers to their knees. It is reminiscent of a Hot Fudge Sundae but in pastry form. It comes from the talented hands of Chef Amy Crowns.

Roll out pie crust and fit into bottom of 9-inch pie pan; set aside.

In a heavy medium-size saucepan melt butter and chocolate over low heat. Transfer to large mixing bowl of electric mixer. With mixer on medium speed, gradually beat in 1 cup sugar until sugar is dissolved. (If mixture firms up, don't be concerned. The addition of eggs will smooth it out.)

Add 2 eggs, beating well after each addition. Beat in 1 teaspoon vanilla, flour and ½ cup walnuts. Pour into pie crust. Sprinkle with remaining 1 cup walnuts.

In a separate bowl, with electric mixer, whip together syrup, remaining ½ cup sugar, 2 eggs and 1 teaspoon vanilla and pour over chocolate batter.

Bake in preheated 350° oven for 45 minutes to 1 hour or until surface is lightly browned and pie has a solid jiggle when moved. Serve room temperature.

THE VINTAGE
3110 8th Street South
Wisconsin Rapids, Wisconsin

Old Fashioned
Sour Cream Blackberry Pie

makes 8 servings

1 unbaked pie crust (9-inch),
　　homemade or purchased
　　refrigerated crust
4 cups fresh blackberries*
1 cup flour
1½ cups sugar
1 cup dairy sour cream

Buy fresh blackberries from a farm market or along a roadside stand for this time-treasured classic that bakes and tastes like warm berries and cream.

Roll out crust and fit into 9-inch pie pan. Pour blackberries into crust, distributing evenly over surface. Set aside.

In a medium bowl, combine flour and sugar with whisk. Add sour cream, stirring to blend ingredients. (Mixture will be thick.) Spoon over blackberries, distributing evenly. Bake in a preheated 350° oven for 1 hour or until top is golden brown. Serve warm; refrigerate any leftovers.

* Raspberries, blueberries, boysenberries, strawberries or peaches may be substituted for blackberries. Adjust sugar amounts according to taste.

THE VINTAGE *Encore*
3110 8th Street South
Wisconsin Rapids, Wisconsin

Wisconsin Cheese Pie
with Apple Cider Marmalade

makes 1 pie

Cheese Pie:

6 ounces cottage or ricotta
cheese
1 package cream cheese (8
ounces), softened
¾ cup sugar
½ teaspoon vanilla
1½ teaspoon grated lemon zest
2½ tablespoons fresh lemon
juice, strained
2 eggs, slightly beaten
1 unbaked pie shell (9-inch
diameter)
Whipped cream—garnish
Fresh berries—garnish

Marmalade:

1¼ cups firm apples, cored and
slivered (unpeeled)
1 tablespoon apple cider
4 teaspoons powdered pectin
2 tablespoons grated orange zest
2 tablespoons grated lemon zest
1¾ cups sugar

THE OLD RITTENHOUSE INN
301 Rittenhouse Avenue
Bayfield, Wisconsin

*According to owners Mary and Jerry
Phillips, this is the most popular pie
served at the Old Rittenhouse Inn. It
reminded me of a lovely lemon-scented
cheesecake and can be served with or
without the Apple Cider Marmalade
glaze. Use any leftover glaze as a garnish with pork entrees.*

In a large mixing bowl with electric
mixer, combine cheeses, sugar, vanilla,
lemon zest and juice. Blend until smooth.
Fold in slightly beaten eggs. Pour into pie
shell.

Bake in a preheated 350° oven for 30
minutes. Completely cool on wire rack before serving.

Make Apple Marmalade by processing
apples in food processor bowl fitted with
metal blade until apples are finely minced.

Place apples, cider, pectin and zests in
medium heavy saucepan. Bring mixture to a
rolling boil. Add sugar and stir until completely dissolved. Return to rolling boil.
Boil for 65 seconds, stirring constantly.

Remove mixture from heat. Cool for 3
minutes; then skim off any foam. Cool
completely. Use 1 cup to glaze cheese pie;
refrigerate remaining marmalade to serve
with pork chops.

Garnish cooled pie with whipped cream
and fresh berries.

Kitchen Table Cheesecake

makes 16 servings

Crust:

1 cup flour
½ cup cold unsalted butter, cut in
    cubes
2 tablespoons sugar

Filling:

1½ pounds cream cheese, room
    temperature
1 cup cottage cheese
1 cup dairy sour cream
4 large eggs
1½ cups sugar
2 tablespoons fresh lemon juice,
    strained
1 teaspoon vanilla
3 tablespoons cornstarch

Topping:

2 cups dairy sour cream
3 tablespoons sugar
½ teaspoon vanilla

A classic New York style cheesecake with incredible smoothness and bound-to-please flavors. Do make this in advance of serving to allow the flavors to "age."

To make crust, place flour, cubed butter and sugar in large food processor bowl fitted with a metal blade and process until mixture forms lumps, about 30 seconds. Press into bottom and halfway up sides of an ungreased 10-inch diameter springform pan. Bake in preheated 350° oven for 13-15 minutes or until golden brown on the edges.

Make filling by combining all ingredients in food processor bowl and process until smooth, about 2 minutes. Pour into baked crust. Bake at 350° for 1 hour or until set in center.

While cheesecake bakes, prepare topping by whisking together sour cream, sugar and vanilla. Spread topping evenly on top of hot cheesecake and return to oven for 10 minutes more.

Remove from oven and cool in pan on wire rack to room temperature. Remove sides of springform pan. Cover top with plastic wrap. Refrigerate overnight. Cheesecake must "age" at least 8-12 hours before serving. This keeps for 5 days under refrigeration.

THE KITCHEN TABLE
East 3rd and Maple
Marshfield, Wisconsin

Wisconsin Cranberry and Granny Smith Apple Bread Pudding Cake

with Grand Marnier Cream

makes 14 servings

Bread Pudding Cake:

7 tablespoons unsalted butter (divided)
8 large eggs
1¼ cups sugar
1 quart milk
1 cup heavy whipping cream
3-4 tablespoons vanilla
1 teaspoon ground cinnamon
1 teaspoon ground nutmeg
6 French Pistolet Rolls (3-inch diameter) or 1 baguette (about 1 pound) sliced ½-inch thick
½ cup raisins
1 cup cranberries
1 cup peeled and diced Granny Smith apples
½ cup pecans, chopped

Orange Cream:

3 tablespoons Grand Marnier liqueur
2 tablespoons sugar
1 teaspoon vanilla
2 cups heavy whipping cream
½ cup freshly squeezed orange juice (about 1 orange)
1 teaspoon grated orange zest

FANNY HILL
3919 Crescent Avenue
Eau Claire, Wisconsin

Chef John Mazzei works wonders with his interpretation of a bread pudding suited for royalty. It is baked and unmolded for its pretty fruit-studded, layered presentation. And the Orange Cream Sauce might just be addictive.

Butter a *tight-fitting* 10-inch diameter by 2½-inch deep springform pan with 1 tablespoon butter. Line bottom with parchment paper; set aside.

In a large mixing bowl with electric mixer on medium, cream eggs and sugar well, about 3 minutes. Add milk, cream, vanilla, cinnamon and nutmeg; mix well.

Carefully line bottom of pan with sliced bread pieces, at least ½-inch thick. Fill in all holes by tearing bread into cubes. (This is very important so pan does not leak.) Sprinkle half of the raisins, cranberries, apples and pecans over bread layer.

Pour 2½ cups of egg mixture over fruit layer and pat well with fingers to make sure all bread is totally soaked. Repeat bread layer and sprinkle remaining half of fruits over bread and add one more layer of bread cubes. Fill in all holes. Pour remaining egg mixture on top and let soak in refrigerator for 2 hours until all egg mixture is absorbed.

Sprinkle remaining 6 tablespoons butter, cut in small pieces, over top. Bake in a Bain Marie (water bath)—a deep dish pizza pan works well for this—in preheated 350° oven for 1½ hours.

While pudding bakes, make orange cream by heating Grand Marnier, sugar and vanilla in small heavy saucepan over medium heat for 1 minute. Whisk in cream, orange juice and zest. Reduce until slightly thickened, about 20 minutes.

Serve pudding warm with orange cream, a dollop of whipped cream and a fresh mint leaf, if desired. Leftover pudding cake and cream should be refrigerated. Pudding may be warmed for 20 seconds on full power in microwave.

Strawberry Amaretto Torte

makes 12 servings

Sponge Cake:

6 large eggs, room temperature
1 cup sugar
1 cup flour, sifted
¼ cup unsalted butter, melted
⅓ cup amaretto liqueur plus 1
    tablespoon (divided)

Filling:

2 pints fresh strawberries,
    rinsed, drained
½ cup sugar plus 2 tablespoons
    (divided)
2 pints heavy whipping cream
    (divided)

HARBOR VIEW CAFE
First and Main
Pepin, Wisconsin

A recipe for strawberry season developed by Cook Judy Krohn that is composed of multi-layers of amaretto laced sponge cake, filled with homemade strawberry puree and whipped cream. The cake can be baked ahead for ease in preparation.

Make sponge cake by beating eggs in large mixing bowl with electric mixer until foamy. Add sugar gradually, beating until sugar is dissolved, about 10 minutes.

Quickly fold in butter and flour. Pour batter into two greased and floured 9-inch diameter pans. Tap pans on counter to remove large air bubbles. Bake at once in 350° oven until lightly browned and top springs back when gently touched with finger, about 20-25 minutes.

Cool in pans for 5 minutes on wire rack; then turn out on racks to cool completely. Layers may be wrapped and refrigerated until ready to use.

Two hours before serving, cut each cake layer horizontally into 2 layers and sprinkle all four layers with ⅓ cup amaretto liqueur.

Reserve 12 nice strawberries with hulls for garnishing. Crush remaining strawberries in bowl of food processor fitted with metal blade with ½ cup sugar. Place berries in saucepan and bring to boil over medium heat and boil until thick and jamlike, about 12 minutes. Chill in refrigerator until cold.

In a deep, non-plastic bowl, using chilled beaters, whip 3 cups heavy whipping cream until stiff, 3-4 minutes or until beaters leave spiral pattern in cream. Fold chilled strawberry mixture into whipped cream, blending thoroughly.

Place 1 cake layer cut side up on large cake plate. Spread with one-fourth of strawberry/cream mixture. Repeat layers and filling, ending with strawberry cream mixture. Set in refrigerator to chill.

Whip remaining 1 cup whipping cream in deep non-plastic bowl with electric mixer until cream is stiff, about 3 minutes. Add 2 tablespoons sugar and 1 tablespoon amaretto liqueur. Frost sides of torte with flavored whipped cream, reserving ½ cup cream to pipe rosettes with a star tip in a pastry tube around top of cake.

Cut torte into 12 servings with large knife dipped in water between cuts. Garnish each torte serving with a whole strawberry.

Dagobert Chocolate Truffle Cake

makes 12 servings

Sponge Cake:

4 tablespoons unsalted butter,
   clarified*
1 teaspoon vanilla extract
½ cup plus 1 tablespoon sifted
   cake flour
⅓ cup plus 1 tablespoon sifted
   unsweetened cocoa powder
4 large eggs
⅔ cup sugar

Syrup:

1 cup granulated sugar
⅓ cup water
2 tablespoons Grand Gala or
   other orange-flavored liqueur

Ganache:

½ cup heavy whipping cream
1⅞ cups (15 ounces) milk
1¾ pounds semisweet chocolate,
   chopped
6 ounces unsalted butter,
   softened

Guests at the American Club may well remember this ethereal creation of Pastry Chef Richard Palm. It is one of the desserts showcased in the annual December event, "In Celebration of Chocolate," hosted by the American Club and its staff of talented chefs headed by Executive Chef Rhys Lewis. Tender chocolate sponge cake layers infused with orange-flavored liqueur alternate with thin coatings of smooth ganache. A culinary dream-come-true for chocolate lovers.

To make cake, preheat oven to 350°. Prepare 9-inch round cake pan by lining bottom of pan with parchment paper cut to fit bottom. Spray all of cake pan with vegetable oil spray.

*To make clarified butter, melt 4 tablespoons butter in small saucepan over low heat. When completely melted, remove from heat, let stand for about 5 minutes allowing the milk solids to settle to the bottom. Skim the foamy white butterfat from the top; discard. Spoon off the clear yellow liquid and reserve—this is the clarified butter. Set aside. Discard the milk solids on the bottom of the pan. You should have approximately 3 tablespoons clarified butter for this recipe.

THE AMERICAN CLUB
Highland Drive
Kohler, Wisconsin

Combine hot clarified butter and vanilla in small bowl; keep warm. Sift flour and cocoa twice. In a large heatproof mixing bowl, whisk eggs and sugar. Place bowl in a saucepan over barely simmering water. Heat to lukewarm, whisking occasionally. Remove bowl from heat. Beat egg mixture at high speed with electric mixer, until it has cooled, tripled in bulk and resembles softly whipped cream.

Sift about one-third of flour mixture over whipped eggs. Fold with spatula, quickly but carefully. Fold in one-half of remaining flour mixture; then the other half.

Fold in hot butter mixture; fold completely. Turn batter into prepared pan. Bake until center of cake springs back when touched gently, 20-25 minutes. Cool cake in pan on wire rack before unmolding. Chill cake in refrigerator before cutting.

In a small heavy saucepan make syrup by combining sugar and water and bring to boil over medium heat. Stir constantly until sugar is completely dissolved. Remove from heat; chill in refrigerator until cold to the touch, about 1 hour. Stir in liqueur when chilled. Set aside.

In a small heavy saucepan make ganache by bringing cream and milk to boil over medium heat. Add chopped chocolate and stir in gently until melted. Add butter; stir until smooth. Cool until firm at room temperature.

Slice cooled 9-inch sponge cake into 3 layers. Brush each layer with chilled syrup—do not soak. (Reserve any extra syrup for other uses.) Place layer of ganache on top of each layer. Using the remaining ganache, pipe lattice on top using a star tip in a pastry tube.

Chocolate Symphony

makes 1 chocolate cake 9¼" x 5¼" x 1½" high

White Chocolate Mousse:

6 ounces white chocolate,
  chopped
2 tablespoons vegetable oil
2 tablespoons water
½ teaspoon unflavored gelatin
1 cup heavy whipping cream
2 tablespoons light rum

Dark Chocolate Mousse:

6 ounces bittersweet chocolate,
  chopped
2 tablespoons vegetable oil
1 cup heavy whipping cream
2 tablespoons light rum

Chocolate Glaze:

6 ounces bittersweet chocolate,
  finely chopped
½ cup heavy whipping cream
1 tablespoon light corn syrup

RED CIRCLE INN
N44 W33013 Watertown Plank Road
Nashotah, Wisconsin

This is an elegant and sinful chocolate dessert that can be made ahead. The mousse and cake can be layered and frozen for up to two weeks. Just glaze when needed, allowing 2 hours ahead of time to thaw cake before completing. Don't let the length of the recipe frighten you. The instructions from Pastry Chef Cheryl Poweleit are precise and detailed for beginning or experienced cooks.

To make cake layer, bake *one-half* of your favorite chocolate cake recipe in a 9¾" x 6" x 1¾" baking pan. (If in a hurry, you could use one-half of any chocolate cake mix. Mix and bake according to package instructions.) Turn out of pan onto wire cooling rack; cool completely placing in refrigerator until cold to the touch. With a sharp knife cut cake to measure 9¼" x 5¼" x 1½".

Line a 9¼" x 5¼" x 1¾" loaf pan with plastic wrap, leaving a 2-inch overhang over top of the 2 long sides. Smooth out wrinkles.

Make white chocolate mousse by melting white chocolate until smooth in top of double boiler over hot, *not simmering* water. Transfer chocolate into a large bowl. Stir in oil. Put water in a small, heat-proof cup. Sprinkle gelatin over water and let stand 5 minutes. Place the cup in a saucepan with just enough water to come halfway up side of cup. Heat in pan with hot water, stirring just until dissolved, 2 to 3 minutes. Transfer gelatin mixture to a small bowl.

In a chilled bowl with chilled beaters, beat together cream and rum until it begins to form soft mounds. *Do not over whip the cream.* Whisk about ½ cup of cream into gelatin until smooth. Scrape gelatin/cream mixture back into bowl of cream; whisk briefly. Fold ⅓ of gelatin into white chocolate to lighten, then fold in remaining gelatin/cream. Scrape into loaf pan and smooth top with spatula. Place level in freezer to chill.

Make dark chocolate mousse by melting the same way as for white chocolate. Stir in oil. Whip cream and rum together until it forms soft mounds. Fold ⅓ of whipped cream into chocolate to lighten. Fold in the remaining whipped cream. Scrape into loaf pan over white chocolate mousse and even layer with spatula.

Top with cake layer; wrap the plastic over top. At this point you can freeze for up to 2 weeks. If you do not freeze it, allow it to set in freezer at least 30 minutes before you remove it from the pan.

To remove the cake, gently loosen the plastic wrap from the pan. Turn upside down; tap the top of the pan. Place on a wire cooling rack on a baking sheet. Place in the freezer while preparing the glaze.

Make glaze by placing finely chopped chocolate in a medium bowl. Set aside. In a small saucepan, combine the cream and syrup. Cook over medium heat until it just comes to a boil. Pour over the chocolate; let stand 30 seconds. Gently whisk until smooth, trying not to create any air bubbles. Allow to stand at room temperature until tepid and slightly thickened.

Remove the cake from freezer. Pour glaze over top, using a spatula to quickly spread glaze evenly over top and sides. Allow the glaze to set up in the refrigerator for at least 15 minutes. Transfer to serving tray. Serve immediately. (If symphony was frozen, allow to thaw in refrigerator 2 hours before serving.) Cut into 10 slices and garnish with fresh fruit, whipped cream or mint leaves.

Lime and Toffee Tart

makes 10-12 servings

Crust:

¾ cup unsalted butter, room
  temperature
¼ cup plus 2 tablespoons sugar
1 small egg, room temperature
¼ teaspoon vanilla extract
Pinch of salt
1¾ cups plus 2 tablespoons flour

Filling:

1¼ cups sugar
1 cup unsalted butter, room
  temperature, cut into pieces
1 cup fresh lime juice
11 large egg yolks
1 tablespoon plus 1½ teaspoons
  grated lime peel

Toffee Sprinkles:

1 cup sugar
1 cup water
2 tablespoons heavy whipping
  cream
3 tablespoons unsalted butter,
  cut in pieces

SANFORD RESTAURANT
1547 North Jackson
Milwaukee, Wisconsin

Sweet and tart come together in this beautiful citrus dessert from Chef Sanford D'Amato that can be prepared one day in advance of serving and then refrigerated. Add the toffee sprinkles right before serving.

To make crust, cream butter with sugar in medium bowl with electric mixer until light, stopping occasionally to scrape down sides of bowl. Beat in egg, vanilla and salt. Add flour and stir until dough comes together in a ball.

Roll out dough between two sheets of waxed paper to ¼-inch thickness. Peel off top sheet of paper. Invert dough onto 11-inch diameter tart pan with removable bottom. Peel off top sheet of paper. Press dough into pan; trim edges. Refrigerate until well-chilled, about 1 hour.

Bake crust in preheated 350° oven until golden brown (about 23-25 minutes) piercing with fork, if dough puffs. Transfer to wire rack and cool completely in pan.

To make filling, bring sugar, butter, lime juice, egg yolks and peel to boil in heavy large non-aluminum saucepan over medium heat, whisking constantly. Boil just until thickened, about 5 seconds. *Do not overcook or mixture will curdle.* Pour filling into prepared crust. Refrigerate until set, about 4 hours. This can be prepared one day ahead.

To make toffee sprinkles, lightly oil a 15-inch x 10-inch baking sheet; set aside. In a heavy medium saucepan, cook sugar and water over low heat, stirring occasionally until sugar dissolves, about 4 minutes.

Increase heat to medium/high and bring to a boil, without stirring, until sugar turns caramel color, about 8 minutes. Remove from heat. Carefully stir in cream, then butter (mixture will bubble vigorously). Stir until butter melts.

Pour onto prepared baking sheet. Freeze toffee until firm, about 20 minutes. Break toffee into 2-inch pieces. In the bowl of a food processor fitted with metal blade, coarsely chop toffee using Pulse/Off button. Toffee can be prepared in advance. Store in airtight jar in freezer.

Remove tart from pan. Transfer to platter. Sprinkle with toffee sprinkles and serve.

White Chocolate Raspberry Tart

makes 8-10 servings

Crust:

1¾ cups flour
¼ cup sugar
½ teaspoon salt
12 tablespoons unsalted butter
2 large egg yolks
1-2 tablespoons cold water
  (divided)

Filling:

1½ cups fresh or frozen dry pack
  raspberries
½ cup sugar
1½ tablespoons cornstarch
2¼ cups white chocolate chips
1 tablespoon solid vegetable
  shortening
6 tablespoons unsalted butter,
  room temperature
12 ounces cream cheese, room
  temperature
1 teaspoon vanilla

Topping:

½ cup semisweet chocolate chips
2½ tablespoons unsalted butter

THE INN AT CEDAR CROSSING
336 Louisiana Street
Sturgeon Bay, Wisconsin

*Some recipes in their very first read-
ing just say "delicious" and this one,
from Pastry Chef Jeanne Demers, is
definitely one of them. If you are strongly biased in favor of chocolate and raspberry combinations, I suggest you begin
on this dessert at once. Fresh raspberries are desirable but not required. Dry
pack frozen berries work just as well.*

In a large mixing bowl, combine flour,
sugar and salt. Cut in butter with pastry
blender until mixture is crumbly and resembles cornmeal.

Add 1 tablespoon water to egg yolks and
whisk slightly. Add to flour mixture and
mix until dough holds together. (Add the
remaining 1 tablespoon water if necessary.)
Form dough into a ball and roll out on
lightly floured surface until large enough to
line an 11-inch diameter x 1-inch high tart
pan with removable bottom. Trim off excess
dough after lining tart pan leaving ½-inch
extra dough around rim. Fold excess ½-inch
dough down over top of rim to strengthen
edge. Smooth to even edges.

Line the tart pan with parchment paper
or foil and fill with dried beans or pie
weights. Bake in preheated 350° oven for 15
minutes. Remove beans or weights and bake
5 minutes longer. Remove pan to cool on
wire rack. Set aside.

In a small saucepan combine raspberries, sugar and cornstarch and cook over medium heat until thickened, stirring frequently. Cool. Spread raspberry mixture over bottom of prebaked tart. Refrigerate until set, about 1 hour.

While tart cools, melt white chocolate in small heavy saucepan over low heat with shortening, stir until melted. Set aside.

In a medium bowl, combine the softened butter and cream cheese with electric mixer until very smooth. Add vanilla. On low speed of mixer continue beating cheese mixture and slowly add white chocolate mixture until chocolate is totally incorporated. Spread mixture over cooled raspberry layer, smoothing the top.

In small heavy saucepan melt semisweet chocolate chips and remaining 2½ tablespoons butter over low heat until smooth and blended. Place chocolate mixture in a pastry bag with a number 3 or 4 round tip. Pipe stripes about ¾-inch apart across the tart. Immediately run a knife through the chocolate in ¾-inch lines to feather the chocolate. (It helps to have dark chocolate melted and in bag so that lines can be piped and feathered right away before white chocolate sets up.) Refrigerate until firm.

Chocolate Hazelnut Truffles

makes about 3 dozen

1½ pounds semisweet chocolate,
  chopped coarsely
½ cup heavy whipping cream
3 tablespoons Frangelico liqueur
½ cup unsweetened cocoa
  powder
2 teaspoons ground cinnamon
About 36 hazelnuts (filberts)

These lovely, little morsels from Chef Case Van Kleef have a surprise buried inside their chocolate interiors. You could roll these in finely chopped hazelnuts as well.

Put chocolate in top of double boiler. Place top of double boiler over bottom pan which has 1 inch of simmering water in it. Melt chocolate over low heat, stirring until smooth.

Add the cream and liqueur; stir until well blended. Cool the mixture to room temperature, then beat with a portable mixer at medium speed until fluffy, about 2-3 minutes. Cover pan with layer of paper towel. Refrigerate until firm, about 1 hour.

Meanwhile, combine cocoa powder and cinnamon in a small bowl. Set aside. When truffle mixture is chilled, use your hands to form about 36 ¾-inch diameter balls around the hazelnuts.

Roll each ball lightly in the cocoa mixture; then place on tray and chill until firm, about 2-3 hours. Keep truffles chilled and covered in storage. Best eaten when fresh.

THE COTTAGE
1502 Post Road
Plover, Wisconsin

Chef's Helper

As I edited recipes for *Encore* Wisconsin, I kept a list of terms and techniques that I felt should be explained in the context of the cookbook. They are things you may or may not know, depending on your cooking experience. But they are things you will need to know in order to ensure the success of the chefs' recipes in this volume. And reading through them may just be a nice little refresher course in the art of cooking.

Al dente. A gauge for cooking perfect pasta, which translated means "to the tooth." Perfectly cooked pasta should be pleasant to the tooth—not too soft, not too chewy—almost a bit underdone.

Andouille sausage. A smoked, spicy pork sausage originally of French origin that is associated with New Orleans dishes. It is cooked and ready-to-eat and used frequently to accent or flavor dishes like Gumbo.

Bain marie. I had been doing this process for years, calling it a water bath. It means the same thing but bain marie sounds prettier. Basically, a shallow pan containing warm water is used to hold other smaller containers with sauces, soups or mixtures that require even temperatures to cook or bake in the oven slowly without burning or curdling. Many bread puddings, custards and like dishes ensure their creamy smooth texture by using a bain marie. In general, water should never exceed half the height of the vessel containing sauce or other ingredients.

Beurre manie. A hand butter made by mixing together equal parts of flour and cold butter with your hands until butter is totally incorporated into the flour. This hand butter may then be whisked in small amounts into a hot liquid for use as a thickener.

Blanching. A means of par-cooking vegetables which helps retain their color and some of their crispness—done by plunging vegetables into boiling water for a short period of time and then immediately submerging in ice water to stop the cooking process.

Bouquet Garni. A small bundle of herbs, often parsley, thyme and bay leaves, wrapped in cheesecloth and added to a soup or stew for flavor.

Brown sugar. The recipes don't specify this because I believe it is understood. But perhaps a reminder is necessary. Brown sugar must always be measured *packed*.

Butterflied. To deeply slash a fillet of meat lengthwise down the center without cutting through the meat in order to double the surface area of the meat and make cooking more even. Butterflied loins can be done by your butcher at time of purchase. If in doubt about the cut, have the butcher demonstrate the process. Butterflied loins are often stuffed and then rerolled before roasting.

Chiffonade cut. A way of cutting salad greens or herbs that involves tightly rolling the leaves together and slicing the rolls into uniform thin ribbons. The effect is very pretty.

Chinois. A conical strainer with a handle, having a very fine mesh screen for straining broths and jellies. If one is not available, a very fine double screen strainer will work.

Clarified Butter. Clarified butter is often specified by chefs. It allows butter to be heated to a higher temperature without burning. Begin by using slightly more butter than the amount of clarified butter required for the recipe. For example, 8 tablespoons butter will yield about 7 tablespoons clarified butter.

Melt butter in small saucepan over low heat. When completely melted, remove from heat; let stand for about 5 minutes allowing the milk solids to settle to the bottom. Skim the foamy white butterfat from the top; discard. Spoon off the clear yellow liquid and reserve—this is the clarified butter. Set aside. Milk solids on the bottom of the pan may be used over vegetables.

Court Bouillon. A spiced aromatic liquor or stock used mainly for cooking fish and shellfish. Wine and vinegar may sometimes be added to the court bouillon which is prepared in advance to extract the flavors of the ingredients before the fish is added.

Cracked black pepper. Coarse, freshly ground black peppercorns frequently used in salad dressings.

Creme Fraiche. A French dairy product that uses cream with the addition of a lactic bacteria culture that thickens the cream and makes it somewhat tart without souring it. It is similar in taste and texture to sour cream. Unlike sour cream, Creme Fraiche can be heated to high temperatures without curdling. It is available in specialty stores.

Deglaze. Heating stock, wine or liquid together with the browned bits and cooking juices left in a pan after sautéing or roasting in order to make a sauce or gravy. Liquid is cooked until all the pan juices have been dissolved in the liquid, thereby adding flavor and color. Some recipes may call for straining the liquid after deglazing.

Demi-glace. A rich brown sauce (Espagnole) which is reduced to the nth degree and which has the addition of a white stock, such as veal, and a Madeira, sherry or similar wine. Its rich and intense flavors add complexity to any dish. There is no substitute for demi-glace.

(Divided). This term at the end of a listed ingredients alerts the cook that this ingredient will be divided into parts for its use in the recipe. For instance, 1 cup of unsalted butter, (divided) may mean that ½ cup is used to make a cake batter and the remaining ½ cup to make a topping for the cake. Read the recipes carefully and note the divided amounts used in each part. (Maybe you will want to underline them before you begin. I do and it helps me avoid mistakes.)

Emulsion. A mixture obtained by incorporating one kind of liquid (drop by drop) into another liquid. Vinaigrettes are examples of emulsions. Emulsified sauces such as hollandaise, beurre blanc and bearnaise have butter as their principal ingredient. They need to be made carefully as the directions specify. They are subject to separation if they are mixed too quickly or cooked over too high temperatures or allowed to stand too long.

Espagnole Sauce. A basic brown sauce which is used as a base for a number of other brown sauces. It is made with a brown stock to which a brown roux and a mirepoix (a mixture of diced vegetables cooked very gently and used to enhance the flavor of meat, fish or game dishes or sauces) have been added followed by the addition of a tomato puree.

Flan. An open tart filled with fruit, a cream or a savory mixture which may be served as a hot entree or as a dessert. In France or Spain is also used for a caramelized egg custard that is made in a mold, turned out and served cold.

Flour. Recipes use all-purpose flour unless otherwise specified.

Frenched. A process often done by butchers in preparation of a rack of lamb for roasting. It refers to the removal of excess fat and scrap meat on the top edge of lamb ribs prior to roasting.

Galette. Originally a flat round cake of variable size. But in this collection, the galette is not sweet but composed of finely sliced vegetables, butter and seasonings that are bound together with a light sauce, arranged in compressed rounds in a baking pan, baked and then unmolded for serving.

Hot Peppers. Cautionary notes are added to recipes using hot peppers in this cookbook. The safest way to handle hot peppers in food preparation is with plastic or rubber gloves. Do not touch eyes or skin during preparation. Wash hands thoroughly with soap and water when finished with hot peppers.

Julienne cuts. Lengthwise cuts of vegetables, generally about 1½ inches long and ⅛-inch thick that are also called shoestring cuts or matchstick cuts. They are often required in stir fries (favored in many Far East dishes), also salads and vegetable dishes. The uniformity of the cut allows perfectly even cooking and presents itself beautifully on a plate or in a bowl. You need a sharp knife and patience for this process.

Large Eggs. This is the size preferred and used by most chefs. In one or two recipes, either a small egg or extra large egg will be specified. For best results, use exactly what the chef requests. (You could remove a small portion (¾ teaspoon) of either large egg yolk or white in order to get the equivalent of a small egg or add a bit to a large egg yolk or white to get an extra large.)

Lemon juice. Use only freshly squeezed and strained lemon juice in the recipes in this book. The same is true for any recipe using lime juice.

Light Ingredients. Be advised that substituting light sour cream for regular sour cream or light butter or any other fat or calorie reduced product in place of the original product reduces the fat content of the dish, affecting the water content of baked products and the way sauces thicken. Additional ingredient adjustments may be necessary. If dietary concerns are a part of your cooking, any substitution with reduced fat and calorie products should be regarded as experiments, with variable results.

Malibu liqueur. A clear, spiced rum liqueur used in tropical drinks.

Mandoline. A stainless steel or plastic kitchen gadget with very sharp blades that allows the cook to slice or julienne vegetables in a variety of thicknesses—very quickly. Knuckle guards are included and they are a necessity for safe use. Prices vary from to $32.95 to $175.00 (depending on the base material used) at kitchen and cookware supply stores.

Non-reactive. A stainless steel, enamel, glass or tin-lined cookware that does not affect the taste of the foods cooked in it. The term is often interpreted to mean a non-aluminum utensil.

Olive Oil. Buying olive oil can be an ordeal for the novice cook. The colors are different, the flavors vary and so do the prices. Generally speaking, the highest priced and best flavored oils are those that are labeled *extra virgin* or *superfine virgin* and are coldpressed, extracted from the olives without heat or chemicals. These are the ones generally preferred in vinaigrettes. Lower cost and lightly flavored oils are usually labeled *pure* or simply *olive oil* and are used for sautéing.

Pinbone. The obvious larger bones in a fish fillet that occur at regular intervals along the length of the fillet. They can be removed with a needle-nose pliers or even sometimes pulled out by grasping the bone ends using a piece of paper towel and pulling briskly.

Prosciutto. A special air cured ham available at specialty markets.

Refrigerated Pie Crusts. I find the Pillsbury brand of pie crust in the refrigerated section of supermarkets to be most satisfactory if the cook is pressed for time or doesn't like to make pie crusts.

Rice sticks. These are thin, brittle white noodles made from rice powder. If they are used in stir-frying, they must be softened in liquid first. If they are deep-fried, they puff up crisp and are used as a garnish. You will find them in the Oriental sections of most supermarkets.

Room Temperature. Some ingredients require room temperature in order to achieve their greatest volume like beaten egg whites and butter in a creamed mixture. Use care when letting foods come to room temperature as perishable foods will not store safely at room temperature.

Roux. A cooked mixture of equal amounts of flour and fat used to thicken sauces. The length of cooking time varies depending on the color of roux desired—a white roux should be cooked until it just begins to take on a golden color. A brown roux is cooked long enough to get a light brown color.

Sea salt. A clean, distinctive salt from the sea made by evaporation of sea water rather than mined. It is often preferred by chefs because it does not mask the flavor of food. It has a less chemical taste than common table salt and less is generally required to flavor foods.

Sous Chef. Second in charge in the kitchen under the Executive Chef.

Toasted nuts (seeds). This process adds flavor to any variety of nuts. Spread nuts on a baking sheet in a single layer and toast in a preheated 350 degree oven for 4-5 minutes or until nuts turn golden brown and become fragrant. Remove from baking sheet and spread out to cool on a clean cutting surface.

Unsalted butter. Butter labeled as such which contains no salt and is generally preferred by chefs. All recipes in this cookbook, unless otherwise specified, use unsalted butter. It has a fresher, somewhat sweeter flavor than salted butter. But because salt acts as a preservative, unsalted butter is more perishable than salted butters. Unsalted butter stored in the refrigerator should be used within two weeks for freshest flavors. Excess unsalted butter may be wrapped securely and frozen.

Vinaigrette. A basic dressing for salads or vegetables that can also be used as a marinade for meats, poultry, seafood and fish. It is composed of oil, acid (vinegar or citrus juice), salt and pepper. Additional ingredients such as Dijon-style mustard, fresh herbs and other seasonings are common additions. Made by whisking salt (or other seasonings) in bowl with acid and then slowly whisking in oil in a slow stream until mixture thickens and forms an emulsion.

Zest. The outer, colored part of the rind on citrus fruit. Be sure you grate or strip off only the colored outer layer, not the bitter white membrane that lies next to the zest.

Contributing Restaurants

52 STAFFORD—AN IRISH GUEST HOUSE
52 Stafford Street
Plymouth, Wisconsin 53073
(414) 893-0552
Hours: Sunday through Thursday 5pm-9pm (dinner); Friday and Saturday 5pm-10pm (dinner); Saturday 11:30am-2pm (lunch).
Reservations: Advised
Payment: All major credit cards accepted
(66, 121)

THE AMERICAN CLUB
Highland Drive
Kohler, Wisconsin 53044
(414) 457-8000
The American Club resort hotel houses four restaurants: The Immigrant for fine dining, The Horse & Plow for casual fare, The Wisconsin Room for breakfasts and elaborate buffets, and the Greenhouse dessert and ice cream parlor.
Hours: Vary by restaurant; dining is available at the hotel between 6am and midnight (seasonal).
Reservations: Reservations vary by restaurant. Reservations are required in the Immigrant; not required in the Horse & Plow; recommended for the Wisconsin Room and not required for the Greenhouse.
Payment: Options include check, MasterCard, Visa, American Express, Discover, Diner's Club
(148)

BENNY'S KITCHEN
239 West Main Street
Waukesha, Wisconsin 53186
(414) 544-9359
Hours: Tuesday through Friday 11am-2pm (lunch); Tuesday through Saturday 5pm-9pm (dinner); Sunday 11am-2pm (lunch). Closed Mondays.
Reservations: Suggested
Payment: MasterCard, Visa
(55, 74)

BERNARD'S
701 Second Street North
Stevens Point, Wisconsin 54481
(715) 344-3365
Hours: Open 7 days a week from 4pm.
Reservations: Appreciated
Payment: MasterCard, Visa
(117)

BODER'S ON THE RIVER
11919 North River Road
Mequon, Wisconsin 53092
(414) 242-0335
Hours: Tuesday through Sunday 11:30-2pm (lunch); Tuesday through Thursday 5:30pm-8:30pm (dinner); Friday and Saturday 5:30pm-9:30pm (dinner); Sunday 4pm-7pm (dinner). Closed Mondays.
Reservations: Suggested
Payment: All major credit cards accepted
(38)

THE BOULEVARD INN
925 East Wells Street
Milwaukee, Wisconsin 53202
(414) 765-1166
Hours: Monday through Thursday 11:30am-9pm; Friday and Saturday 11:30am-10:30pm; Sunday 10:30am-9pm.
Reservations: Required
Payments: All major cards accepted
(42)

CAFE KNICKERBOCKER
1030 East Juneau Avenue
Milwaukee, Wisconsin 53202
(414) 272-0011
Hours: Monday through Saturday 6:30am-11:30pm; Sunday 9am-10pm, brunch from 9am-3pm.
Reservations: Recommended for dinner
Payment: MasterCard, Visa, no personal checks
Patio: Seating for 70 during summer season
(26, 73, 108)

CAFE MOZART
311 West Main Street
Durand, Wisconsin 54736
(715) 672-4103
Hours: Closed January. Tuesday through
    Saturday 11:15am-2:30pm (lunch), 5pm-
    9pm (dinner).
Reservations: Recommended on weekends
    for dinner
Payment: Personal checks with
    identification accepted
(67, 126)

CARVERS ON THE LAKE
RESTAURANT AND INN
N5529 County Trunk A
Green Lake, Wisconsin 54941
(414) 294-6931
Hours: Summer hours: Tuesday through
    Sunday from 5pm. Winter hours:
    Wednesday through Sunday from 5pm.
Reservations: Recommended
Payment: MasterCard, Visa, personal check
(36, 104)

THE CHESTERFIELD INN
BED & BREAKFAST
20 Commerce Street
Mineral Point, Wisconsin 53565
(608) 987-3682
Hours: Tuesday through Saturday 8am-9pm;
    Sunday 12am-5pm (brunch), 5pm-9pm
    (dinner).
Reservations: Suggested
Payment: MasterCard, Visa, American
    Express
(77)

CHRISTIE'S
PAPER VALLEY HOTEL
& CONFERENCE CENTER
333 West College Avenue
Appleton, Wisconsin 54913
(414) 733-8000
Hours: Monday through Friday 11:30am-
    2pm (lunch), 5:30pm-9pm (dinner);
    Saturday and Sunday 5:30pm-9pm
    (dinner).
Reservations: Advised
Payment: All major credit cards accepted
(18, 122)

CITY STREETS
RIVERSIDE RESTAURANT
712 Riverfront Drive
Sheboygan, Wisconsin 53081
(414) 457-9050
Hours: Monday through Friday 11am-2pm
    (lunch); Monday through Thursday 5pm-
    9pm (dinner); Friday and Saturday 5pm-
    10pm (dinner). Closed Sundays.
Payment: MasterCard, Visa, American
    Express
(16)

CLUB CHA CHA
1332 West Lincoln Avenue
Milwaukee, Wisconsin 53215
(414) 385-3344
Hours: Monday through Friday 11:30am-
    2:30pm (lunch); Sunday through Thursday
    5:30pm-10:30pm (dinner); Friday and
    Saturday 5:30pm-11:30pm (dinner).
Reservations: Accepted for parties of 5 or more
Payment: Master Card, Visa, American
    Express
(24, 62)

THE CLUBHOUSE
ON MADELINE ISLAND
P.O. Box 880
Bayfield, Wisconsin 54814
(715) 779-5010
Hours: Dinner hours are always 6pm-10pm.
    Days open change with months: May,
    June, October—Friday, Saturday, Sunday;
    July, August—Wednesday through
    Sunday; September—Thursday through
    Sunday.
Reservations: Advised
Payment: MasterCard, Visa
(14, 22)

CONTINENTAL CAFE
19035 West Bluemound Road
Waukesha, Wisconsin 53186
(414) 786-9095
Hours: Monday through Thursday 7am-
    9pm; Friday and Saturday 7am-10pm;
    Sunday 9am-2pm (brunch).
Reservations: Accepted for parties of 5 or more
Payment: Checks, MasterCard, Visa, Diner's
    Club
(33)

THE COOKERY
4135 Main Street, Hwy. 42, P.O. Box 376
Fish Creek, Wisconsin 54212
(414) 868-3634
Hours: Open daily from 7am through
  October. Winter weekend hours: Friday
  and Saturday 7:30am-8pm; Sunday
  7:30am-4pm.
Reservations: Not accepted
Payment: MasterCard, Visa
(51)

THE COTTAGE
1502 Post Road
Plover, Wisconsin 54467
(715) 341-1600
Hours: Monday through Friday 11:30am-
  2pm (lunch); open 7 days a week for
  dinner 5pm-10pm.
Reservations: Accepted
Payment: MasterCard, Visa, Discover,
  American Express, Diner's Club
(156)

CRANDALL'S RESTAURANT
640 West Washington Avenue
Madison, Wisconsin 53703
(608) 255-6070
Hours: Monday through Thursday 11am-
  9pm; Friday 11am-10pm; Saturday 11am-
  2pm (lunch), 4:30pm-10pm (dinner);
  Sunday 10am-2pm.
Payment: MasterCard, Visa, American
  Express, Discover
(12)

THE CREAMERY RESTAURANT
AND INN
County Trunk C, P.O. Box 22
Downsville, Wisconsin 54735
(715) 664-8354
Hours: Sunday 10am-2pm (brunch), 4:30pm-
  8pm (dinner); Tuesday through Saturday
  11:30am-2pm (lunch); Tuesday through
  Thursday 5pm-9pm (dinner); Friday and
  Saturday 5pm-10pm (dinner). Closed
  Mondays.
Reservations: Not accepted
Payment: Personal checks accepted
(124)

FANNY HILL
3919 Crescent Avenue
Eau Claire, Wisconsin 54703
(715) 836-8184
Hours: Tuesday through Sunday 5pm-9pm
  (dinner).
Reservations: Recommended
Payment: MasterCard, Visa, American
  Express, Discover, personal checks
(144)

GASTHAUS RESTAURANT
2720 North Grandview Boulevard
Waukesha, Wisconsin 53188
(414) 544-4460
Hours: Monday through Friday 11:30am-
  2pm (lunch); Monday through Friday
  5pm-10pm (dinner); Saturday 5pm-10pm
  (dinner); Sunday 4pm-9pm (dinner).
Reservations: Recommended
Payment: MasterCard, Visa, American
  Express
(80)

THE GRANARY
50 West 6th Street
Oshkosh, Wisconsin 54901
(414) 233-3929
Hours: Monday through Friday 11am-2pm
  (lunch); dinner daily from 5pm. Dinner
  ends Sunday through Thursday at 10pm,
  Friday at 10:30pm, Saturday until 11pm.
Reservations: Appreciated
Payment: MasterCard, Visa, American
  Express, Discover
(120)

GRENADIER'S RESTAURANT
747 North Broadway at Mason
Milwaukee, Wisconsin 53202
(414) 276-0747
Hours: Monday through Friday 11:30am-
  2:30pm (lunch); Monday through Saturday
  5:30pm-10:30pm (dinner). Closed Sundays.
Reservations: Recommended
Payment: All major credit cards accepted
(46, 58, 105)

HARBOR VIEW CAFE
First and Main
Pepin, Wisconsin 54759
(715) 442-3893
Hours: Thursday, Friday, Saturday and
Monday 11am-2:30pm (lunch); Thursday,
Friday and Saturday 5pm-9pm (dinner);
Monday 5pm-8pm (dinner); Sunday noon-
7:30pm. Closed Tuesdays and Wednesdays.
Reservations: Not accepted
Payment: No credit cards accepted but
checks are accepted
(146)

HEAVEN CITY RESTAURANT
S91 W27850 National Avenue
Mukwonago, Wisconsin 53149
(414) 363-5191
Hours: Monday through Friday 11:30am-
2pm (lunch); Monday through Saturday
5:30pm-10pm (dinner); Sunday 5pm-9pm
(dinner).
Reservations: Suggested
Payment: All major credit cards, except
Discover
(25, 50, 92)

THE INN AT CEDAR CROSSING
336 Louisiana Street
Sturgeon Bay, Wisconsin 54235
(414) 743-4200
Hours: Summer hours: 7am-9pm seven days
a week. Winter hours: 7am-8:30pm seven
days a week.
Reservations: Not accepted Friday and
Saturday evenings in summer, otherwise
accepted
Payment: MasterCard, Visa, Discover,
personal checks
(30, 34, 82, 128, 154)

JACOBI'S OF HAZELHURST
9820 Cedar Falls Road, P.O. Box 308
Hazelhurst, Wisconsin 54531
(715) 356-5591
Hours: Tuesday through Sunday 4:30pm-
10pm (dinner). Closed Mondays.
Reservations: Suggested
Payment: MasterCard, Visa
(45)

KARL RATZSCH'S
OLD WORLD RESTAURANT
320 East Mason Street
Milwaukee, Wisconsin 53202
(414) 276-2720
Hours: Monday through Friday 11:30am-
10pm; Saturday 11:30am-11:30pm; Sunday
11am-10pm (brunch 11am-3pm).
Reservations: Recommended
Payment: All major cards accepted
(95)

THE KITCHEN TABLE
East 3rd and Maple
Marshfield, Wisconsin 54449
(715) 387-2601
Hours: Monday through Saturday 7am-2pm
(breakfast and lunch).
Reservations: Not accepted
Payment: No credit cards accepted but
personal checks are accepted
(47, 78, 143)

LARA'S TORTILLA FLATS
715 North Main Street
Oshkosh, Wisconsin 54901
(414) 233-4440
Hours: Monday through Saturday 11am-
10pm; Sundays 4pm-9pm.
Reservations: Suggested
Payment: MasterCard, Visa, American
Express, Diner's Club, Carte Blanche
(13, 19, 90)

L'ETOILE
25 North Pinckney
Madison, Wisconsin 53703
(608) 251-0500
Hours: Monday through Thursday 6pm-
8:30pm; Fridays and Saturdays
5:30pm-9:30pm.
Reservations: Strongly recommended
Payment: MasterCard, Visa, personal checks
(52, 68)

MAIN STREET BISTRO
340 Main Street
Racine, Wisconsin 53401
(414) 637-4340
Hours: Monday through Friday 11am-
  2:30pm (lunch); Saturday 11am-3:30pm
  (lunch); Monday through Thursday 5pm-
  10pm (dinner); Friday and Saturday 5pm-
  11pm (dinner). Closed Sundays.
Reservations: Strongly suggested
Payment: MasterCard, Visa, American
  Express, Diner's Club
(17)

MARIA'S ITALIAN CUISINE
159 West Wisconsin Avenue
Oconomowoc, Wisconsin 53066
(414) 569-9393
Hours: Monday through Saturday 11:30am-
  2pm (lunch); Monday through Thursday
  5pm-10pm (dinner); Friday 4:30pm-10pm
  (dinner); Saturday 5pm-10pm (dinner).
  Patio Dining for 50 is available in season.
Reservations: Accepted for parties of 6 or
  more every night except Friday
Payment: MasterCard, Visa
(87)

NORTON'S MARINE DINING ROOM
South Lawson Drive
Green Lake, Wisconsin 54941
(414) 294-6577
Hours: Summer hours: Monday through
  Friday 11:30am-2:30pm (lunch); Saturday
  and Sunday 11am-3pm (lunch); Monday
  through Saturday 5pm-10pm (dinner);
  Sunday 4:30pm-10pm (dinner). Call for
  winter hours.
Payment: MasterCard, Visa, American
  Express
(114)

THE OVENS OF BRITTANY
1718 Fordem Avenue
Madison, Wisconsin 53704
(608) 241-7779
Hours: Monday through Sunday 7am-10pm
Reservations: Suggested
Payment: MasterCard, Visa, American
  Express
(81)

THE OVENS OF BRITTANY
305 State Street
Madison, Wisconsin 53703
(608) 257-7000
Hours: Monday through Saturday 7am-
  9:30pm; Sunday 8am-9:30pm
Reservations: Suggested for dinner
Payment: MasterCard, Visa, American
  Express
(37)

THE OLD RITTENHOUSE INN
301 Rittenhouse Avenue
Bayfield, Wisconsin 54814
(715) 779-5111
Hours: May through October 5:30pm-
  9:30pm (dinner). November through
  April: Friday, Saturday and Sunday
  5:30pm-9:30pm (dinner).
Reservations: Recommended
Payment: MasterCard, Visa, personal check
(88, 137, 142)

QUIVEY'S GROVE
6261 Nesbitt Road
Madison, Wisconsin 53719
(608) 273-4900
Hours: Lunch (Stone House) Tuesday
  through Friday 11:30am-2pm. Dinners
  (Stone House) 5:30pm -9:30pm every
  evening. Stable Tap & Grill open daily
  from 11am-10pm. Closed on all major
  holidays.
Reservations: Not accepted in Stable Tap
Payment: MasterCard, Visa and personal
  checks
(40, 59, 65, 84, 94)

RED CIRCLE INN
N44 W33013 Watertown Plank Road
Nashotah, Wisconsin 53058
(414) 367-4883
Hours: Tuesday through Sunday from 5pm
  (dinner). Garden and patio reception
  facilities are available 7 days a week for
  groups from 20-300.
Reservations: Welcomed, suggested on
  weekends
Payment: MasterCard, Visa, American
  Express
(29, 43, 71, 119, 125, 150)

RED GERANIUM RESTAURANT
7194 Highway 50 R
Lake Geneva, Wisconsin 53147
(414) 248-3637
Hours: Summer hours: Monday through
Saturday 11:30am-2:30pm (lunch); Monday
through Thursday 5pm-10pm (dinner);
Friday and Saturday 5pm-10:30pm
(dinner). Sunday 10am-3pm (plated
brunch); 4pm-9pm (dinner). Call for
winter hours.
Reservations: Advised during summer
season
Payment: MasterCard, Visa
(100)

THE RESTAURANT
1800 North Point Drive
Stevens Point, Wisconsin 54481
(715) 346-6010
Hours: Monday through Saturday 5pm-9pm
(dinner).
Reservations: Recommended
Payment: MasterCard, Visa, American
Express
(72, 111)

RIVER WILDLIFE
Kohler, Wisconsin 53044
(414) 457-0134
River Wildlife is a private club open only to
members and their guests, or registered
guests of the American Club resort hotel
who have purchased a daily entrance pass.
Hours: Monday through Saturday 11am-
1:45pm (luncheon); Sunday 11:30am--
1:30pm (brunch); Friday and Saturday
5:30pm-9pm (dinner).
Reservations: Mandatory
Payment: Member monthly billing.
American Club guests may charge to
room. Also Visa, MasterCard and Discover
Cards are accepted.
(110)

THE SANDHILL INN
170 East Main Street, Hwy. 78
Merrimac, Wisconsin 53561
(608) 493-2203
Hours: Summer hours: Tuesday through
Sunday 5:30pm-10pm (dinner); Sunday
9:30am-2pm (brunch). Winter hours:
Tuesday through Saturday 5:30pm-10pm;
Sunday 9:30am-2pm (brunch). Closed
Mondays.
Reservations: Recommended
Payment: MasterCard, Visa, American
Express
(99, 131, 132, 134)

SANFORD RESTAURANT
1547 North Jackson
Milwaukee, Wisconsin 53202
(414) 276-9608
Hours: Monday through Thursday 5:30pm-
9pm (dinner); Friday and Saturday
5:30pm-10pm (dinner).
Reservations: Required
Payment: MasterCard, Visa, American
Express
(20, 102, 152)

STOUT'S LODGE
ISLAND OF HAPPY DAYS
Red Cedar Lake
Mikana, Wisconsin 54857
(715) 354-3646
Hours: Open May 1; close November 1 for
guest season; dinner menu changes daily
Reservations: Required
Payment: MasterCard, Visa
(61, 75, 96)

SUSIE'S RESTAURANT
146 Fourth Avenue
Baraboo, Wisconsin 53913
(608) 356-9911
Hours: Tuesday through Saturday 8am-3pm;
Friday and Saturday 5pm-9pm (dinner);
Sunday 8am-1pm (brunch). Closed
Monday.
Reservations: Appreciated for dinner
Payment: Personal checks
(31, 60, 106, 138)

SWEETWATERS
1104 West Clairemont Avenue
Eau Claire, Wisconsin 54701
(715) 834-5777
Hours: Sunday through Thursday 11am-
10pm; Friday and Saturday 11am-11pm.
Reservations: Weekend reservations advised
Payment: MasterCard, Visa, American
Express, Discover, also personal checks
(54)

THE VINTAGE
3110 8th Street South
Wisconsin Rapids, Wisconsin 54494
(715) 421-4900
Hours: Monday through Friday 11am-2pm
(lunch); Monday through Sunday 5pm-
10pm (dinner).
Reservations: Advised
Payment: MasterCard, Visa, American
Express
(35, 39, 98, 116, 118, 130, 140, 141)

THE WHITE APRON
414 Maple Drive
Sister Bay, Wisconsin 54234
(414) 854-5107
Hours: Winter hours: Friday and Saturday
5:30pm-8:30pm (dinner). Summer hours:
Thursday through Sunday 5:30pm-9pm
(dinner).
Reservations: Recommended
Payment: MasterCard, Visa
(56, 57, 76, 86)

THE WHITE GULL INN
4225 Main Street
Fish Creek, Wisconsin 54212
(414) 868-3517
Hours: Monday through Sunday 7:30am-
noon (breakfast); noon-2:30pm (lunch);
5:30pm-8pm (dinner). Fish boils are served
May through October on Wednesday,
Friday, Saturday and Sunday evenings;
November through April on Wednesday
and Saturday evenings. Candlelight
dinners are served on all nights when fish
boils are not served.
Reservations: Requested for dinner
Payment: MasterCard, Visa, American
Express, Discover and Diner's Club
(28, 112, 136)

WILSON STREET GRILL
217 South Hamilton
Madison, Wisconsin 53703
(608) 251-3500
Hours: Monday through Friday 11am-2pm
(lunch), 5:30pm-9:30pm (dinner).
Reservations: Advised
Payment: Visa, MasterCard, personal checks
(48, 64, 70, 129)

Index